Drawing on the insights and disciplines of contemplative spirituality, Tony writes without legalism to help us engage and encounter God through Christ in meaningful ways. This book will significantly widen our worship experience as we present our real selves to a real God.

> *Dave Bilbrough, international songwriter and*
> *worship leader*

This book has been a word spoken in season for me, an answer to the cry of my heart. It verbalises so many of my own feelings and longings about what facilitates intimacy with God. It is helping me as I seek to help others come to a place of stillness where they can rediscover and rest in the love of God. I could not recommend it more highly. If I were to choose one book to give to my friends at the moment it would be this one.

> *Carol Wain, YWAM, Liverpool*

This is one of those books which has had a profound influence on my life. Tony not only reminds us of our need to slow down and simply 'be' with God, he also illustrates how we can do this, by providing practical guidelines on meditation and contemplative prayer. This book can enrich your walk with God.

> *Debbie Lovell-Hawker, clinical psychologist, Oxford*

Jesus called his disciples to be with him. He still does, because our Christian faith is founded on a relationship with him. Tony reminds us of the importance of nurturing that relationship, and helpfully suggests ways in which we can open ourselves to receive the love of God, which is at its centre. I warmly commend this book to all who long to draw closer to God and remain in him.

Mary Salter, Vice-Principal, All Nations Christian College,
England

During the last ten years I have experienced a growing hunger to get closer to the God I tell children about. This book has done two things for me. It has made my hunger more acute, and it has pointed me towards the source of satisfying that hunger. As a result I have given myself permission just to be, rather than to be doing all the time. I have seen the summer sun rise in the Derbyshire hills, just sitting in God's presence. Now I long more than ever to see a younger generation growing up in love with Jesus.

Graham Reed, former General Director, Children
Worldwide, Sheffield

RHYTHMS OF GRACE

The words of Jesus:

Are you tired? Worn out? Burned out on religion?
Come to me. Get away with me and you'll recover your life.
I'll show you how to take a real rest.
Walk with me and work with me – watch how I do it.
Learn the unforced rhythms of grace.
I won't lay anything heavy or ill-fitting on you.
Keep company with me and you'll learn to live freely and
    lightly. (Matthew 11:28–30, *The Message*)

Rhythms of Grace

TONY HORSFALL

KINGSWAY PUBLICATIONS
EASTBOURNE

First published 2004

Rhythms of Grace is a revised and expanded
edition of *The Call to Intimacy*, first published in Singapore
in August 2001 by ShareTheWord.com

Unless otherwise indicated, Scripture quotations are
from the New International Version © 1973, 1978, 1984
by the International Bible Society.
Other versions include *The Message* © Eugene H. Peterson
1993, 1994, 1995 by NavPress, USA.

ISBN 1 84291 133 3

Published by
KINGSWAY COMMUNICATIONS LTD
Lottbridge Drove, Eastbourne BN23 6NT, England.
Email: books@kingsway.co.uk

Book design and production for the publishers by
Bookprint Creative Services, P.O. Box 827, BN21 3YJ, England.
Printed in Great Britain.

Dedication

To Evelyn, my wife and companion on life's journey,
and our children, Alistair and Debbie, who make it so
much more interesting!

To friends at Ackworth Community Church,
for your love and support, and your openness to God.

To colleagues at Bawtry Hall –
thanks for ten very satisfying years, and the opportunity
to grow.

Acknowledgements

My thanks to:

Alan Chew of ShareTheWord.com in Singapore, who first had the vision and faith to publish my work, and who has opened many 'doors' for me.

Joyce Huggett, mentor and guide, and trailblazer in these things.

Angela Ashwin, for her permission to use her beautiful prayers from her books *Wait and See* and *Wait and Trust*, originally published by Eagle.

Beverley Shepherd for The Dream – such a challenging story and fitting ending to this book.

For all those other writers who have inspired me, especially those quoted in these pages, and for permission from their publishers to use their work.

Contents

CONTENTS

Foreword

You've placed a hunger in my heart
To see Your glory,
You've caused a thirst that I cannot ignore;
You've stirred a passion that will
Drive me to Your presence
And I won't rest until
You've heard me cry for more.[1]

That verse from one of Stuart Townend's winsome worship songs describes so accurately the hunger that is gnawing at many hearts in these days when the pace of life seems to accelerate year by year.

I heard that heart-hunger being expressed in both Singapore and Malaysia recently. I have heard it being expressed in England, North America, Australia and New Zealand. I heard it being expressed by the author of this book when he first came to our home to make a retreat towards the end of his sabbatical leave.

During that retreat and since, Tony Horsfall has tasted

---

[1] Stuart Townend, Thankyou Music 1999.

and seen for himself that 'the Lord is good.' Many readers and would-be contemplatives will be grateful to him for the time he has spent sharing with us some of the fruit of his own exploration into a form of prayer that has set him free to enjoy an ever-deepening intimacy with God.

The way the contents of the book have been spread out reminds me of an appetising buffet. Every chapter spreads before us a variety of tempting tit-bits. Sample them and they simply whet your appetite so that you find yourself going back for more – and more, and more. Take Chapter 8, for example. Here we read: 'If we seek him, we shall find him; if we have a longing for him, it will eventually be satisfied.' Such sentences are to be savoured and reflected on. As we reflect, God's Spirit may well stir up in us a desire for more – more stillness, more sustenance, more of God's love, more of God himself.

The author makes this claim: 'When we meet God, we experience beauty – sheer loveliness, tenderness, compassion and grace.' That has been my experience as I have read and prayed through the contents of this book. That is why it is a joy for me to recommend the following pages to those who can no longer ignore or push away the passion for God's presence that has been planted in their hearts by God's Spirit. In particular, I warmly recommend it to those who find their hearts echoing the kind of sentiments that are voiced in Stuart Townend's song but who come from a church background that has never taught or understood the value of a more still approach to God.

As I have read, reread and prayed through each chapter of this book, there have been occasions when I have sensed the anointing of God's Spirit on the insights shared. My prayer as this little gem goes to print is that through its pages and by the grace of God readers will find themselves enriched and enlightened, and that they will be nourished as they feast from the banquet spread before them. Whenever this happens, the author will be rewarded for the hard work he has poured into this book and God will be glorified.

Joyce Huggett

Introduction

'Don't stand still! Keep moving!'

I can still hear the sergeant-major like voice of my physical education teacher booming across the playground. He loved to have us young boys running around on our toes – his own passion for physical fitness expressed in his fierce determination to develop our athletic prowess. No chance of dawdling while he was around! We learned to keep moving, or else!

I guess that much of my adult life has been lived at a similar tempo. The world around us fears to stand still, and so do we. We are drawn into its motion, caught up in its activity, anxious lest we be left behind. Even as a Christian, my life has been lived at pace. There has always been so much to be done, so many needs to be met, so many opportunities, and always so little time. In this modern world, many of us fear to stand still, and are pressurised to keep moving.

Increasingly I have sensed that there must be a better way to live, and that Christianity has more to offer us than a continual treadmill. During the last few years my concern has led me to a growing interest in contemplative spirituality – the kind of Christian tradition that isn't afraid to slow down, and to be still and quiet. Being an activist, and coming from an evangelical/charismatic background, this has led me into unfamiliar territory, but I like what I have seen, and feel there is a great deal to be learned from a more reflective tradition.

Some of my friends laugh at me, and suggest it is to do with my age, the 'stage I'm at' in middle life. Well, maybe there is something in that. Certainly I appreciate a slower pace to life these days, and occasionally feel quite nostalgic! But hopefully my interest is more than symptomatic of a personal transition. It has been aroused, I think, by God, and for at least two conscious reasons.

The first is what I would call a deep hunger to know God more intimately. I am grateful for my background and nurture in evangelicalism over the last 30 years. Through this I came to personal faith in Christ and an assurance of salvation, I developed a love for the Bible and an appreciation of the cross, and I felt a growing desire to share my faith with others and to serve God overseas. It gave me a grounding in the faith, and remains the basis on which I stand.

I am grateful too for my involvement in the charismatic tradition, which opened up to me the working of the Holy Spirit, the joys of praise and worship, and a more experiential faith. Again, I continue to stand firmly and squarely within this stream of Christianity.

In my journey of faith, evangelicalism got me started and the charismatic movement took me further. What I am feeling now is the need to journey on, to find the kind of spirituality that will take me deeper into God. The contemplative tradition seems to offer such a possibility. It provides what I call the third strand in the 'rope' of an integrated approach to Christian spirituality.

As I have begun to experience the contemplative tradition, something inside me is stirring. I am awakening to the
benefits of beautiful, Spirit-filled liturgy, and being surprised by the new appreciation I have for symbolism. I am
learning to rest more, to become more reflective and to hear
God in the stillness. It is as if a long-neglected part of me is
suddenly stirring into life.

Let me explain here that by liturgy I mean structured
forms of prayer as opposed to the extempore kind with
which most evangelicals and charismatics are familiar. I used
to be of the opinion that only prayers prayed off the cuff were
of any value, and that dependency on the written prayers
of others showed a lack of spiritual maturity. I now realise
that the Spirit can use liturgy powerfully in the right context,
and that structured prayer can offer great support to us,
especially in times of spiritual dryness. We need to incorporate both in our corporate worship and devotional life.

More than this, I am finding rich treasures within the
history of the church that I never really knew existed or
which I felt were out of bounds for me because they
belonged to an alien tradition. I am discovering people in
the past who knew great intimacy with God, and who
found it through silence and solitude rather than noise and
activity. And I am realising that within my own tradition I
have never really been taught how to develop my inner life,
to become aware of the life of God within me. I am hungry
to explore this new dimension.

This personal desire to know God is not my only motivation, however. A second conscious reason for exploring
contemplative spirituality is that I believe it provides a
healthy balance to the hectic pace of life at which many
Christians choose to live and the opportunity to begin to
learn how to rest in the love of God.

I have a deep concern for those within the evangelical/charismatic tradition who, like myself, are committed to serving God with their whole being, and who find themselves caught up in a spiral of ever-increasing activity. There is an alarming drivenness about many Christian workers and church leaders. Unless we introduce a quieter and more reflective strand into our spirituality, I fear we will see increasing numbers of our best people sidelined through burnout or breakdown.

I know there is a 'macho' form of Christianity that boasts, 'I want to burn out for God, not rust out', but I don't think such people have ever really seen the damage done to someone through burnout. If they had they would not be so full of bravado. What do they think it means to 'burn out'? And do they think that this is what God wants for his children? I cannot for a moment believe that it is God's will for us to end up physically, mentally and emotionally shattered, or even to live as we do, constantly on the edge – unable to rest, always on the go, rushing from one worthy cause to the next. We urgently need to find some balance in our lives, and that is where I believe the insights of the contemplative tradition can come to our rescue.

I should say that from a personality point of view I do not find contemplative worship and prayer comes easily. I am by nature an extrovert. I like to be busy, I like to be active. I find it difficult to sit and be quiet, and it is hard for me to concentrate for long periods. I seldom want to reflect on what is past, preferring to move on quickly to what is next. It is, however, exactly because of this that I, and the many who are like me, need to build into life some of the spiritual disciplines (the rhythms of grace) associated with a contemplative lifestyle. They will bring balance and richness and give freshness and vitality to a life that could easily become overworked, stale and empty.

I am writing primarily for the many activists within the evangelical/charismatic section of the church. You may be a mission partner energetically serving God in a cross-cultural location. You could be a minister or pastor, busily seeking to build the church in a postmodern world. Or you might be one of that great legion of faithful church members, toiling away tirelessly at the heart of your local congregation. Whoever you are, I want to encourage you to open yourself up to new things, to explore and experiment with tried and tested ways of developing the spiritual life, some of which may be new to you. Above all, I want to encourage you to respond to the voice of the Spirit as he calls us to greater intimacy with God and offers you a place of rest within his all-embracing love.

Nowhere is that call more clearly heard than in the words of Jesus in Matthew 11:28–30. Here the Saviour offers to take our burdens from us, to exchange our wearisome labour for his divine rest. Eugene Peterson's vibrant paraphrase in *The Message* (quoted at the front of this book) expresses exactly the radical nature of what is involved.

Those worn out by constant activity, burned out by the demands of legalistic religion, are invited to find true rest and recovery of life by coming to Jesus. As they enter into relationship with him they discover he is no overbearing taskmaster, but rather one who loves them unconditionally and without reservation. This experience of grace leads them to a place of rest and acceptance, where it becomes natural to want to keep company with Jesus, and to develop a rhythm of life that makes it possible to remain in that love and to grow in intimacy with him. Thus they begin to learn how to live lightly and freely, and how to serve from a place of rest.

Which means a whole new way of living – a way of following Jesus that sounds both attractive and attainable.

Come to Me

The two great gospel words are 'come' and 'go'; the one a word of invitation, the other a word of command. The first speaks of intimacy, the second of activity. Both are important in the Christian life, but our coming to Jesus must always precede our going out from him. For many there has been too much 'going' and not enough 'coming', resulting in lives which are spiritually impoverished and lacking in both depth and passion. At this time the Spirit is reminding us that the gracious invitation of Jesus to intimacy with himself remains his priority and is the foundation of everything else in the Christian life.

1

Invitation to Intimacy

Everyone longs for intimacy.

Whether we are young or old, male or female, we have an in-built need to love and be loved. There is a longing deep within each of us to be known and accepted for who we are, without having to pretend to be what we are not. We yearn for the freedom to be completely ourselves and to know that we are loved, respected and appreciated for who we are. We need to be able to fail and yet feel safe and secure, knowing that our acceptance remains intact, our value undiminished even when our performance falters. We want to know that someone has seen the worst in us and yet loves us just the same. We ache for the freedom that true intimacy brings.

Not surprisingly, most of us expect to find intimacy in human relationships. We assume that through friendship, or marriage, our need for closeness, for unconditional love and acceptance, will be satisfied. Reality, however, tells us a different story.

Of course, human friendships can be sweet and do in part bring a measure of that for which we are yearning. Marriage too brings us closer to the oneness we crave, but even at its best it can never quite deliver that for which our innermost being cries out. Indeed it was never intended to, for this in-built longing for intimacy is in fact a God-given need, created within each one of us to draw us to the Creator of our souls. This is the 'God-shaped vacuum' that Augustine spoke of and which exists within every man, woman and child. Only in relationship with God can our need for intimacy begin to be fully met. Only in the final communion of heaven will it be completely and totally satisfied.

Intimacy is ultimately a spiritual issue because only God can offer the unconditional love that allows us to be ourselves and know that we are accepted and valued as we are. It is expressed in what the Bible calls grace: the unrestrained mercy of God flowing towards undeserving sinners. It means that God is the one who knows the worst about us and loves us just the same.

Our yearning for intimacy is in fact an echo of Eden, for there in the Garden Adam and Eve lived in unbroken fellowship with God day by day, until sin came into the world and spoiled everything. Having been born as descendants of Adam, we begin life out of fellowship with God. The reason Christ came into the world was to give himself as an offering for our sin and to reconcile us to the Father. When by faith we accept the benefits of his saving death we are brought back into relationship with him. Friendship is restored and intimacy can begin.

It is into this living relationship that Jesus invites us, and why he says, 'Come unto me.' The gospel invitation is a call to intimacy, to closeness, to oneness. This is what he is offering to each of us. He presents us with an opportunity to get to know him, to walk with him and to see from close up how he does things. We can learn from him by sharing personally in what he is doing – the most effective teaching method of all.

All this we can do without fear of being taken advantage of or of being abused. Because he is full of grace, and wants only what is best for us, he will never ask of us what we cannot deliver, but will always work with us to ensure we can achieve that which he has planned for us. Neither will he overwhelm us with the demands of legalistic religion. His call is to a relationship based on grace, grounded in his unconditional love for us and guaranteed by the unchanging nature of his character. We do not have to perform to gain his acceptance; we are accepted already. In such a relationship we can find true rest, the freedom to be ourselves and the confidence to be at home in his presence.

Grace therefore leads us to intimacy, and intimacy is what the Christian life is all about. It is a love relationship, and we are called into friendship with the one who is the Lover of our souls. Once we know that God is for us, that we have no need to fear him or to dread his presence, we can approach him with confidence, and intimacy becomes wonderfully possible. All the time we are afraid of him, thinking him to be harsh and demanding, an unpredictable tyrant, we will want to keep our distance. As soon as we discover the depth and wonder of his love for us, we long to be with him, to know him more fully.

This understanding that the Christian life is essentially a love story is thoroughly biblical and totally transforming. God is the divine Lover and we are his beloved, and the drama of redemption is the story of his relentless love seeking us out. Of course he has plans and purposes for us, but they are the plans and purposes of lovers. Those who are one of heart inevitably share the same desires. Christian service, whether in terms of world mission, social involvement or evangelism, is the inevitable outward expression of intimacy with a God whose love touches the whole world. It is not, however, the reason for the relationship. The relationship is at heart one of love, and without that, service becomes duty and obligation, and is robbed of its passion and delight. If we forget this, our relationship with God will be nothing more than a business transaction, an employer–employee contract, when all the time God is looking for an explosive love affair.

Brent Curtis and John Eldridge have captured the essence of this in their excellent book *The Sacred Romance*.[1] As the title suggests, their intention is to call the church back to the heart of God and the discovery of the passionate nature of his love for us, so that we can learn to live again the adventure of faith from our hearts. Too many of us live from the outer life of duty ('I ought to') instead of from the inner life of desire ('I want to'), because we have substituted activity for intimacy. As far as these authors are concerned, while in every heart there is a longing for a sacred romance, most Christians have lost the life of their heart and with it their romance with God:

> [F]or many of us, the waves of first love ebbed away in the whirlwind of Christian service and activity, and we began to lose the Romance. Our faith began to feel more like a series of problems that needed to be solved or principles that had to be mastered before we could finally enter into the abundant life promised us by Christ. We moved our spiritual life into the outer world of activity, and internally we drifted.[2]

---

[1] Brent Curtis and John Eldridge, *The Sacred Romance* (Thomas Nelson, 1997).
[2] *Ibid.*, p. 7.

Their analysis of the situation is an accurate one, and perhaps you can identify with it. We are too busy for love. Life in general is busy, and the Christian life has become just as hectic, increasing the tempo at which most of us live and leaving little time to develop our relationship with God. Intimacy in any relationship needs time to develop; spiritual intimacy, and the cultivation of our inner life, is exactly the same. Like a couple who drift apart because they never have quality time together, many of us are in danger of drifting away from the Lover of our souls. We have no time to talk, no opportunity to enjoy each other.

Notice the irony of the situation. It is the 'whirlwind of Christian service and activity' that is the root of the problem. Somehow we have shifted the emphasis away from the inner life to the outer life, from being with God to being busy for him. It is a subtle and plausible trap, for many churches applaud busyness and hyperactivity as spiritual zeal. In their eagerness to achieve their goals and reach their growth targets, individuals can sadly become expendable and spiritual depth can be regarded as a luxury. Extreme busyness becomes a mark of distinction, stress a badge of honour. As Tom Sine has noted, we are in danger of drowning in a sea of busyness.[3]

This was brought home to me when I was leading a seminar in Singapore for a group of church leaders. The topic was 'Staying Spiritually Fresh' and about 30 had gathered together. In the minutes before we began, I noticed one pastor talking animatedly into her mobile phone. She made no effort to relate to any of the other pastors there, but instead made one call after another for about ten minutes. Then, as soon as the seminar started, her head

---

[3] Tom and Christine Sine, *Living on Purpose* (Monarch, 2002), p. 8.

dropped to the table and she fell asleep! Feeling concern for her, I hoped to speak with her afterwards, but immediately we finished she shot out of the room, dashing to her next appointment!

Clearly some find a sense of self-worth in being busy, and even church leaders can derive their identity from their work rather than from Christ. To be busy makes us feel important, but we can be busy doing the wrong things, and miss that which is most strategic. 'We miss God's best,' says Sine, 'because we have little sense of how to find a direction and a rhythm for our lives that flows directly out of our faith.'[4]

This over-emphasis on the outer life that so characterises contemporary church life means that we have few people who can help us understand and explore the inner life. Other traditions have a history of spiritual direction and mentoring, but in the evangelical and charismatic context we have developed expertise in the more pragmatic expressions of our faith, such as how to build a bigger church or how to develop seeker-sensitive services. These are important, but it does mean that we may need to look outside our own traditions if we are to learn about intimacy with God and become skilled at helping people develop their inner life. What is encouraging, however, is the growing hunger in many to be more at home in the inner life; to know how to abide in Christ and how to receive God's love for themselves. Soul care is increasingly on the agenda, as is the longing for intimacy.

There is an awakening amongst many believers today who are no longer satisfied with the hustle and bustle generally known

---

[4] Tom and Christine Sine, *Living on Purpose* (Monarch, 2002), p. 9.

as the Christian life. Call it the deeper life, the contemplative life, or whatever you will. By any name this quality of Christian life is conceived in divine intimacy and born in quiet moments spent between two lovers. Many Christians who are dissatisfied with the emptiness of the noise are hearing His gentle call to something deeper, richer.'[5]

This is the divine invitation that Jesus issues when he says, 'Come to me.' He sees the need of his people even today. Many are tired. Large numbers are worn out. Some are burning out or living on the edge of exhaustion. His heart of compassion reaches out, for he knows there is something better, something more. He longs to draw us to himself and surround us with his divine embrace. He longs to introduce us to the rhythms of his grace so that we can recover our lives.

FOR REFLECTION

1. What do you understand by the term 'intimacy', especially as it refers to your relationship with God?
2. How might the idea of the gospel as a sacred romance change the way you understand and live the Christian life?
3. How do you currently nurture your inner life? Are you satisfied with this? If not, what might you do to improve things?

---

[5] Steve McVey, *The Divine Invitation* (Harvest House, 2002), p. 140. Used by permission of Harvest House Publishers, Eugene, OR 97402, USA.

Recovering Life

The contemporary church stands in great need at the moment, probably without realising it. Evangelical and charismatic Christianity has certain strengths, but also some inherent weaknesses.

At a time when spirituality is so popular, what is distinctive about 'evangelical' spirituality and what are the characteristics of 'charismatic' spirituality? What are their strengths and what are their weaknesses? And why is there so much activity, yet so little knowledge of God? What is it that drives so many Christians to be so very busy?

2

Tired and Worn Out?

'SAVED TO SERVE.'

These were the words painted in bold letters on the banner that hung across the front of the church for all to see. Standing just in front of the banner, Pastor Evans was in full flow, challenging his congregation once again in his own inimitable style to a greater commitment and involvement in the church's programme. It was the first Sunday of the new church year, and he felt it essential to rally the troops to greater endeavour.

Halfway towards the back of the building Sue listened as attentively as she could, her head slightly bowed, her body a little tense. She had heard it all before, having been a church member most of her life. As far as she could make out, the key word in the pastor's address was the word 'more' – more time, more money, more meetings, more witnessing, more commitment . . .

Inwardly she groaned. How could she possibly do any more? Sue was one of the most active members in the church. Married to a husband with a busy and demanding job, she had two growing boys to care for and a part-time job of her own. She taught Sunday school, was on the leadership team, and hardly ever missed a Sunday service or home group. What more could she give? Inside she felt tired and drained, even a little defeated.

As her mind began to drift, quite suddenly another thought came to her. 'More,' she mused. 'Yes, there must be more to the Christian life than this. Surely this is not what Jesus meant when he spoke about life in all its fullness. This can't be the abundant life, surely!'

Although she didn't realise it at the time, it was a seed-thought sowed in her mind by the Holy Spirit – a thought that would lead Sue on to an exciting spiritual adventure. From that moment she determined to rediscover the joy of knowing Jesus, even if it meant doing less in the church. Somehow she felt instinctively that she needed more time and space simply to be with Jesus, to find again her first love. A longing to know God more deeply began to well up within her. A spiritual hunger was growing again in her heart that demanded to be satisfied and it surprised even herself. It was the start of something wonderfully new.

Sue is typical of many within the evangelical and charismatic sections of the church worldwide. Committed and involved, they have given their all to serving God, but find themselves like Sue, tired and weary, longing for something more. There seems to be something lacking in our spirituality, for the way many of us currently practise the Christian life leads us more to activity than to intimacy. The result seems to be that many of us endure our faith rather than enjoy it, for it brings us increasingly into the busyness of the outer life, and less and less into the vitality of the inner life. Worn out by this constant demand for effort, we let go of our anchorage in the love of God and lose the joy of simply knowing Jesus. It all becomes too serious, too pressurised, too exhausting.

It is worth pausing for a moment to consider our own spirituality and how it is expressed. It could be that there is something inadequate in our basic understanding of how to live the Christian life. It is not my intention to be critical here, but rather to examine the approach to Christian living that many of us have enthusiastically adopted without realising it may not provide us with the whole story.

'Christian spirituality' is based on the central teachings of Christianity and describes the way it is practised in everyday life. Essentially it is about how we care for our 'soul' or 'spirit', and the means by which we maintain and develop our relationship with God. David Gillett, in *Trust and Obey*, says it has to do with 'how we articulate our relationship with God in Christ, and the particular practical ways which we find most helpful in developing this relationship from within the whole range of Christian tradition and experience'.[1]

The shape of our spirituality is influenced by many variables, such as our theology, denominational background and personality, and the historical setting in which we live.[2] This means that there are many 'types' of Christian spirituality. So it is that we speak of 'evangelical' spirituality, or 'charismatic' spirituality or 'contemplative' spirituality. Each adjective gives us a clue as to the particular style or form of Christianity that is being practised.

---

[1] David K. Gillett, *Trust and Obey – Explorations in Evangelical Spirituality* (DLT, 1999), p. 6.
[2] For a discussion on the identification of particular 'types' of Christian spirituality, see Alister E. McGrath, *Christian Spirituality: An introduction* (Blackwell, 1999), ch. 2. Also Bradley P. Holt, *A Brief History of Christian Spirituality* (Lion, 1993).

What then is evangelical spirituality?

Some may object to the idea that evangelicalism represents only one 'type' of spirituality, preferring to think that it represents a fully biblical approach to living the Christian life, and is therefore innately superior to other traditions. However, most writers on Christian spirituality objectively see it as one important expression among several.

Some like to identify evangelicalism with the Protestant Reformation of the sixteenth century, while most date its emergence from the evangelical revival of the eighteenth century and the influence of people like Wesley and Whitefield. Evangelicalism is usually described as having four central features: the place of the Bible, the centrality of the cross, personal conversion, and active service.[3]

Since evangelicals regard the Bible as the inspired and infallible word of God, it is not surprising that they place such a great emphasis on the Scriptures and recognise them as the primary way in which he speaks to us. This shows itself in the primacy of expository preaching, the practice of daily Bible reading, the formation of Bible study groups and the custom of seeking to evaluate everything by whether it is 'biblical' or not.

They emphasise the centrality of the cross as the means of salvation and the focus of devotion. A substitutionary

---

[3] For an analysis of the essential characteristics of evangelicalism see: David K. Gillett, *Trust and Obey – Explorations in Evangelical Spirituality* (DLT, 1999), ch. 1; Alister E. McGrath, *Christian Spirituality: An introduction* (Blackwell, 1999), pp. 18–19; James M. Gordon, *Evangelical Spirituality*, (SPCK, 1991) p. 7. The latter looks at evangelicalism through the writings of 22 leading evangelicals from the eighteenth century to the present day.

view of the atonement is usually accepted, whereby Christ is said to have died in the place of the believer, and there is a challenge to live a life worthy of the one who died in our place. 'To be gripped by Calvary love and to be motivated by it, is the very heartbeat of evangelical spirituality.'[4]

Personal conversion is the way into the kingdom of God, and is emphasised as opposed to nominalism; that is, having only the external name of being a Christian. Individuals must be 'born again' and have their own encounter with God. This experience of repentance from sin and of faith towards God is essential for salvation. Individualism is a distinguishing mark of the evangelical approach to Christian living.

The emphasis on service and evangelism (sharing one's faith with others) follows naturally. A deep sense of obligation lies at the heart of evangelicalism, releasing a dynamic of energy to be involved in the cause of Christ. Evangelicals are people who are active for God, whose faith affects the way they live.

In his own helpful appraisal David Gillett adds two other characteristics to those already mentioned. He highlights the emphasis on assurance. Evangelicals believe that it is possible to know with certainty that we are saved. This assurance affects the atmosphere of faith in which we live, giving confidence in God's promises, boldness in prayer and the certainty of heaven and eternal life.

Gillett also mentions the pursuit of holiness. For evangelicals, the goal of living is to become like Christ and to express that Christ-likeness in daily life. There are divergent views as to how this is to be achieved, but holiness of life is a common aim. Sometimes this has led to a confusion of holiness with

---

[4] David K. Gillett, *Trust and Obey – Explorations in Evangelical Spirituality* (DLT, 1999), p. 78.

respectability, and middle-class values as gospel norms. It can sometimes also become legalistic and moralistic.

What about charismatic spirituality?

The charismatic movement in Britain began in the late 1960s, and was strongest in the 70s and 80s. Most parts of the world were affected by the associated renewal movement, and most denominations were touched. It is now generally accepted that, after an initial period of stormy opposition, the evangelical church has largely welcomed renewal and embraced the charismatic emphasis. As Dave Tomlinson says in his book *The Post-Evangelical*, 'It is now clear that the whole centre ground of evangelicalism has become charismaticized.'[5]

Many of the theological and spiritual roots of the charismatic tradition are the same as those of evangelicalism, and of course many of those who embraced the new movement would describe themselves as first and foremost evangelicals. Charismatic spirituality would therefore build on the foundations we have already described, but add some new features and modify some of the old.

Charismatic spirituality would be distinguished by praise and worship, baptism in the Spirit, ministry gifts in the church today, power evangelism and spiritual warfare.

Charismatic renewal brought a new emphasis on praise and worship, and more demonstrable expressions of love for Jesus and fellow believers. This is sometimes parodied

---

[5] Dave Tomlinson, *The Post-Evangelical* (Triangle, 1995), p. 15. He gives a penetrating analysis of the state of the evangelical church today, although I do not agree with all his conclusions or suggestions for the way forward.

as being 'happy-clappy' and 'huggy-feely'! Associated with this, there has been an explosion of new worship songs and a multiplication of worship bands and worship leaders.

Charismatic experience is centred on the baptism or filling of the Holy Spirit and the availability of spiritual gifts for today. In particular the gift of speaking in tongues is valued, and also prophecy, especially personal words from God on behalf of individuals.

Leadership in charismatic churches usually recognises the ministry gifts, such as apostles and prophets, mentioned in Ephesians 4:11 and regarded as being operational in the church today. A church that is being soundly built will normally include apostolic 'covering' and prophetic 'input' to ensure it has good foundations.

Although always present in Pentecostalism, it was the ministry of John Wimber in particular that gave the charismatic emphasis to power evangelism, bringing the ministry of healing and deliverance and 'signs and wonders' back into prominence. Times of 'ministry', when individuals receive prayer for personal needs, are now common in many churches.

A final noteworthy characteristic of charismatic spirituality would be the responsibility to engage in spiritual warfare, based on the victory of Christ on the cross over Satan and demonic powers, and his ascension to a place of rule at God's right hand. This has brought into prominence the ministry of intercession, prayer marches, identificational repentance and spiritual mapping.

So where are we now?

This blending of the evangelical emphasis and the charismatic approach has brought great good to the church worldwide. Ideally, the combination of an emphasis on the word of God (evangelical) and an emphasis on the Spirit of God (charismatic) should have created a balanced but powerful expression of the Christian faith. However, certain weaknesses remain, and may even be exaggerated by this marriage of traditions. The first of these, in my opinion, is the increasing lack of a first-hand knowledge of God in the church today – by which I mean, not the finding of God, but the intimacy with God that makes a real adult relationship possible, natural and comfortable. For all its emphasis on helping people to discover a personal relationship with God, evangelicalism seems to bring people so far but no further. This is one of the reasons why increasing numbers of people within evangelical churches feel frustrsted, and is a fact highlighted by Dave Tomlinson in *The Post-Evangelical*.

Tomlinson says he has met many people who shared the same feeling – 'the feeling that evangelicalism is supremely good at introducing people to faith in Christ, but distinctly unhelpful when it comes to the matter of progressing into a more "grown up" experience of faith'.[6] A more 'grownup' faith for him means the freedom to question or doubt, with fewer predigested opinions and categorical conclusions. Such openness is essential, he believes, in a postmodern world.

Interestingly enough, he sees the postmodern search for spirituality leading in a particular direction:

The post-evangelical impetus . . . is to search for this fresh sense of spirituality in the symbolic and contemplative traditions of the Church rather than in the New Age movement. Failing to find much evidence of these elements in evangelical

---

[6] Dave Tomlinson, *The Post-Evangelical* (Triangle, 1995), p. 3.

spirituality, it is inevitable that post-evangelicals seek to find them in ancient Celtic Christianity, as well as in aspects of Catholicism and Eastern Orthodoxy.[7]

This is why the integration of some aspects of contemplative spirituality into evangelical church life may enhance our evangelistic potential in the new millennium.

For many people the charismatic movement offered fresh hope of a deepening relationship with God. Gillett suggests[8] that it met the need for assurance which was lacking in many second-generation evangelicals, and he may be correct, for the gift of tongues is a very tangible confirmation of God's presence. However, even charismatic experience can leave one still hungry for God.

The widespread interest in the Toronto blessing, and subsequently in Pensacola, perhaps bears witness to the spiritual hunger in the hearts of many charismatics, especially those in leadership. With almost pilgrimage-like devotion, hundreds visited the two 'shrines' seeking for a deeper experience with God. This very fact alone would seem to testify to the inadequacy of current charismatic spirituality. Can we not find God where we are? Is it really necessary to travel thousands of miles, at great expense, to encounter him?

We have to acknowledge that we have failed to teach people how to find God for themselves. Charismatic spirituality has become increasingly personality-centred and focused on the impartation of truth by a few to the passive majority. So we have a plethora of conferences, celebrations and teaching events, plus audio tapes and videos,

---

[7] Dave Tomlinson, *The Post-Evangelical* (Triangle, 1995), p. 10.
[8] David K. Gillett, *Trust and Obey – Explorations in Evangelical Spirituality* (DLT, 1999), ch. 3.

books and magazines, and now cable and satellite TV. What all this does is to create a second-hand faith, where we think we have absorbed truth simply because we have heard it from someone else. It encourages a dependency culture among believers. Rather than seek God for ourselves, we can tune in or switch on to our favourite preacher and be 'fed' yet again. There is little need to seek God for ourselves because we can receive so much spiritual stimulation from others. As long as the worship is good and the teaching inspiring, we can be seduced into thinking we are deepening our relationship with God. However, the growing gap that exists between belief and behaviour in the lives of many contemporary Christians should alert us to the fact that all may not be as well as it appears.

At the same time, a growing hunger for intimacy with God is emerging among charismatics. Many are instinctively looking for something deeper, something more substantial. Worship songs express a more reflective mood, and leaders openly share their own longing to know God more deeply. Those with a prophetic emphasis would see this as a hunger being created by the Spirit of God, calling the church back into a love relationship with Jesus. The time seems to be right to rediscover some of the ancient paths of the spiritual life.

How can contemplative spirituality help us?

The contemplative tradition encourages us to find an intimate relationship with God through silence and reflection. In this it takes its biblical basis from Psalm 46:10: 'Be still, and know that I am God.' The implications of this verse are clear: (1) we can know God, and (2) the best way to get to know him closely is to be still before him and silent in his presence. In such a context God will reveal himself to us more fully.

The contemplative tradition can teach us, among other things, how to still ourselves and how to value and use silence. It can help us to listen to God and show us how to take in his beauty and his glory. It is about 'being' rather than 'doing'; about resting in God's love and allowing our service to flow out of that place of acceptance. It emphasises becoming rather than achieving, and the focus is on finding our identity as God's beloved children rather than through our success, even in ministry. It is about coming to Jesus, and knowing what to do when we get there.

Within the tradition of the church (mostly hidden from evangelicals and charismatics) are the writings and experience of generations of believers who have trodden this path before us. Their wisdom can enlighten us and guide our path even now, if we have the humility to listen and the hunger to search. They can show us how to develop rhythms of grace that fit the context of the twenty-first century.

I look back over my own Christian experience with deep thankfulness for the way God broke into my life. I was not from a Christian family, but was encouraged to attend Sunday school, and was converted as a teenager. The experience was real and deep, and I wept for my sins and knew the joy of forgiveness through what Jesus had done for me on the cross. I was shown how to read the Bible (with the help of Bible reading notes), encouraged to pray and exhorted to share my new-found faith with others. Soon I desired to give my whole life to God and serve him full time.

I went to Bible college and entered the world of evangelicalism proper. Here I was taught what was 'sound' doctrine and, just as importantly, what was considered 'acceptable' behaviour. It was a challenging and stretching experience, but I gladly embraced the whole package. I met some students at college who clearly had a dimension to their Christian lives that I did not have. They spoke about being baptised in the Spirit, and I began to hunger for a similar experience. Eventually I too was filled with the Spirit and received the gift of tongues. This was in the early days of the charismatic movement, and there was a sense of adventure and excitement about what was happening, even if it was controversial to some.

This experience of the Holy Spirit revolutionised my Christian life and made me more open to whatever God wanted me to do. During my last year at the college I felt an increasing burden for the Chinese people, and eventually, together with my wife Evelyn (another benefit of being at the college!), went out to the island of Borneo (East Malaysia) as a missionary. There followed eight exciting years of church planting in a beautiful country where God was powerfully at work.

We returned to Britain in 1983 with two children and an enriched experience of God. I became the pastor of a charismatic church in the heart of the Yorkshire coalfield. In some ways it was more pagan than Borneo, but God was still at work and the church grew. In 1993 I moved into a training ministry, preparing and equipping others going to serve God overseas.

During more than 25 years of full-time Christian service, the centrality of the word of God and the need for the power of the Spirit have been fundamental to all I have done. I am so grateful for the spiritual nurture I received and for those who have helped me on my spiritual journey. But the journey continues, and I am as excited now as I have ever been. The same hunger to know God more deeply burns in my heart. I still stand on the word of God, and still depend upon the Spirit's power, but from both the word and the Spirit I seem to be hearing the call of God to the kind of intimacy with himself that will require some of the disciplines and insights of the contemplative tradition: to be still, and know God in the stillness.

I believe this is far more than God's call to me alone. It is the call of God to many who are like me – evangelicals committedly serving God, and charismatics enthusiastically seeking his kingdom. The longing for greater intimacy is growing, and the desire for the 'rest of God' is increasing. It is a thirst created by God himself, and he intends to satisfy it. We have come so far, but know the road still stretches on ahead of us.

However, an obstacle stands in our path and prevents many of us from finding intimacy with God. What is it? The busy activism that characterises us and is endemic within evangelical/charismatic spirituality.

FOR REFLECTION

1. How would you describe your own spirituality? What is important to you?
2. Look back over your spiritual journey. What have been the landmarks? Why were they important to you?
3. Do you feel a hunger to know God more deeply? If so, what are you doing to satisfy it?

3

Burned Out on Religion?

> It is a trick of the Devil, which he employs to deceive good
> souls, to incite them to do more than they are able, in order
> that they may no longer be able to do anything. (Vincent de
> Paul)

Evangelicals are busy people. They are always doing something, and delight in activity. They seem to value busyness
and prize commitment. Indeed, the highest compliment is
to be described as an 'active' Christian. For evangelicals,
genuine faith results in energetic service for God. A job
advert in a national Christian magazine seems to sum it up:

> Active congregation requires an experienced, dynamic
> Christian on a part-time basis (20 hrs per week) to consolidate
> the existing pastoral work, and to expand outreach into the
> community.

Pity the person who took that job! I wonder what he or she
would have done with their spare time!

What evangelicals sometimes fail to realise is that such
an energetic spirituality is something peculiar to their own

tradition, and that other quite genuine Christians do not always feel the same need to be busily serving God. What is it about evangelical spirituality that produces such activism?

Evangelical activism

First of all, evangelicals believe in a God who acts.[1] They stress his immanence and involvement in the world rather than his transcendence and mystery, and so expect him to be active; and if God is active, they too must be active. The logic is that if God is committed to action, those who want to be close to him will involve themselves in his plans and purposes. 'God is not simply to be imitated in his holiness, but in his activity.'[2]

The call to service is consequently a prominent note in evangelicalism. As R. A. Torrey said, 'The working Christian is the happy Christian.'[3] The reason why some Christians don't backslide is because they are too busy to do so! C. H. Spurgeon added to this insistence on activity by telling younger ministers, 'Kill yourselves with work, and then pray yourselves alive again.'[4] Thus a tradition of hard work and total involvement has been passed down from one generation of believers to another, with laziness

---

[1] David K. Gillett, *Trust and Obey – Explorations in Evangelical Spirituality* (DLT, 1999), ch. 7.

[2] *Ibid.*, p. 159

[3] R. A. Torrey, *How to Succeed in the Christian Life*, p. 82, quoted by David K. Gillett, *op. cit.*

[4] C. H. Spurgeon, *An All Round Ministry*, p. 272, quoted by David K. Gillett, *op. cit.*

seen as a great sin. D. L. Moody, another father of evangelicalism, is quoted as saying:

> Laziness belongs to the old creation, not the new. There is not
> a lazy hair in the head of a true Christian . . . We cannot work
> for God without love . . . but the moment the love of God is
> shed abroad in our hearts, my friends, we cannot help loving
> Him and working for Him.[5]

The second string in the bow of evangelical activism is
the moral obligation which flows from the cross. We have
already noted the centrality of the cross, and the emphasis
on a substitutionary atonement. Linked with this is a constant appeal to the moral obligation of the cross. As Christ
gave himself for us, so we are to give ourselves to him.
Wesley puts it like this:

> Love so amazing, so divine,
> Demands my soul, my life, my all.

A life of sacrificial service is regarded as the only proper
response to the death of Christ on our behalf. It is this sense
of obligation that provides much of the inner dynamic for
the activism that characterises so much of evangelical life.
The legacy of forgiveness is a debt to love. James Gordon
in *Evangelical Spirituality* sums it up with these words:

> Spirituality is lived doctrine. For Evangelicals that means the
> cross is to be lived. The self-giving love of God in Christ, the
> 'grace unspeakable' of a crucified Lord, ignites within the heart
> of the forgiven sinner such fires of love, gratitude and wonder,

---

[5] James M. Gordon, *Evangelical Spirituality*, (SPCK, 1991), p. 316.

that the only sufficient response is a life of self-expenditure, the total surrender of mind, heart, and will.[6]

A third incentive to be up and doing comes from the desire to share the good news with others. Evangelicals feel a moral obligation to 'spread the word' and are therefore committed to evangelism and missionary endeavour. To some extent this is what Gillett calls an 'assurance-generated dynamism', fuelled by the evangelical belief that you can be sure of your salvation, and so in a position to persuade others. Without such conviction it would be difficult to convince anyone. It is also fuelled by the belief that people without Christ are lost and going to hell. Although not stressed as much nowadays, this understanding has always given added urgency to Christian service as far as evangelicals are concerned.

In this context the call to full-time service has been prominent, leading to the unconscious feeling that anyone who is serious about serving God will leave secular employment and involve themselves (usually for minimum financial reward!) in Christian work. The 'heroes' and 'heroines' of evangelicalism are those, past and present, who have done just that – missionaries and church leaders in particular. For those who have not felt such a call there is always a temptation to feel second rate, and to want to show they are as committed as others by working just as hard for God in their free time.

Not surprisingly, such teaching has created within evangelical churches a culture or ethos of activity. Charismatic renewal has added further fuel to the fire as far as being busy for God is concerned.

---

[6] James M. Gordon, *Evangelical Spirituality*, (SPCK, 1991), p. 328.

Charismatic dynamism

The promise of power for service came as a welcome relief to many evangelicals. Worn out and drained by their constant service for God, and feeling ineffective and unfruitful, the baptism in the Spirit brought welcome respite to those who embraced the renewal movement. However, 30 years on, the evidence is that the charismatic movement has only increased and intensified the pressure to do more.

Charismatic spirituality, along with the Church Growth Movement, encouraged a belief in the possibility of numerical church growth. It has brought to us the importance of vision and strategy, of dreaming dreams about what God can do in our towns and cities. It has encouraged us to think big, to make plans, to have goals, to set ourselves targets. It has filled us with stories of large, successful churches and effective ministries. Church leaders, inspired and motivated by talk of revival and dreaming of similar success, willingly give themselves to work even harder to accomplish their goals and achieve their ambitions. Congregations too are exhorted to commit themselves to such projects and to share the vision. For some, the dream comes true. For the majority, it is simply more treading of the treadmill.

Perhaps more than any other tradition, charismatic spirituality emphasises the part that man plays in working with God. While many Christians claim to believe in the sovereignty of God, in practice most believe everything depends on them. So it is that strengthened by their understanding of the victory of Christ, and their insight into spiritual warfare, many charismatics have turned their attention to world mission. The evangelisation of the nations is seen as a task that can be accomplished 'in our generation'. Now we can identify who are the unreached peoples of the world, we can set ourselves realistic targets. 'The gospel for every person and a church for every people by the year AD 2000' was one such statement of intent. What such bold thinking has done is release into church life an even greater responsibility to work hard and achieve the task. There is a world to be saved and not much time to do it in!

So here we have two spiritual traditions, both emphasising the importance of activity, and each influencing the other, so that those within the two traditions find themselves being constantly encouraged to do more for God. There is nothing intrinsically wrong with any of the emphases we have mentioned. It is their combined effect in increasing the push towards activity that gives concern. After all, what are the outcomes of such teaching in the lives of those who seek sincerely to follow?

There is no doubt that the most serious negative effect is that it produces performance-orientated living. For those of a tender conscience, repeated exhortations to work hard become internalised and lead to a 'drivenness' in behaviour. This means that such individuals feel guilty if they are not busy, and demonstrate an inability to relax or to truly enjoy leisure time. It means they measure their relationship with God by how much they have done for him, and only feel at peace when they think they have done enough to satisfy an ever-demanding God. Ironically, it moves them out of grace-based living (the touchstone of evangelical teaching) into works-based living.

Dr Pamela Evans has helpfully exposed this obsession with doing within the church in her challenging book, *Driven Beyond the Call of God*.[7] She recognises that 'much

---

[7] Pamela Evans, *Driven Beyond the Call of God* (BRF, 1999).

of what passes for Christian fervour is workaholism with a religious gloss'.[8] She goes on to suggest that some forms of Christian activity are actually based on addictive patterns of behaviour, and she calls for us to rediscover a more balanced way of living described by Jesus in Peterson's contemporary translation as the 'unforced rhythms of grace'.

While there are many roots of this drivenness, it seems to me that a major part of the problem is the lack of balance in evangelical/charismatic spirituality. We have a theology of work, but not of rest; of doing, but not of simply being. Dr Evans' closing challenge is pertinent:

> Discovering the 'rhythms of grace' speaks to me of settling into the stride pattern we need in order to stay in step with Him, neither lagging behind nor being driven beyond His call.[9]

It is certainly possible to be doing far more than God ever requires of us.

A second disturbing effect of spiritual activism is that we have no time simply to be still and enjoy God. Indeed, evangelical spirituality can help us create an image of God that is far from attractive. It can generate in our minds a picture of one who is constantly demanding, hard to please, seldom satisfied and never off duty. Such a God is not easy to live with, even if we do call him Father!

Furthermore, in this context prayer itself is seen as work – in fact hard work. Gillett speaks of it as 'the intense energetic activity of evangelical intercessory prayer'.[10]

---

[8] Pamela Evans, *Driven Beyond the Call of God* (BRF, 1999), p. 11.
[9] *Ibid.*, p. 197.
[10] David K. Gillett, *Trust and Obey – Explorations in Evangelical Spirituality* (DLT, 1999), p. 177.

Evangelicals emphasise this form of prayer because it is one of the means by which they get the work done. In order to see God in action we must petition him to come to our aid. More than in any other tradition, intercessory prayer is exalted as the most important form of prayer. It involves praying out loud, with great fervour and seriousness and for long periods of time. The idea of silent, contemplative prayer, of relaxing in God's presence and simply being with him without asking for anything, seems strange to many evangelicals:

> Personal spiritual growth may well be a by-product of this central evangelical prayer activity, but cultivation of one's own relationship with God is not the purpose of prayer as it is in some other traditions.[11]

A third and serious negative effect can be found in the damage to health, well-being and relationships that results from over-active lifestyles. There seems to be a culture that says this is the price we pay; this is how we show we are committed. Increasing numbers of Christian workers are stressed out and suffering health problems. Marriages are breaking down, children are growing rebellious. Meanwhile, many are leaving the ministry, and others are dropping out of the church, no longer able or willing to pay the price. Few seem willing to question this; few seem willing to stand up and say, 'Wait a minute. This can't be right!' Organisations and churches go on demanding more and more from their people, not realising that they are driving them into the ground.

In the midst of it all though, the still, small voice of God

---

[11] David K. Gillett, *Trust and Obey – Explorations in Evangelical Spirituality* (DLT, 1999), p. 172.

can be heard, calling us back to balance and to integration of quieter, more reflective ways. David Ellis, at the time UK director of the Overseas Missionary Fellowship, made such a call in a very brave article called appropriately 'Why we may need to do less for God'.[12] He likens some Christian workers to the workaholic, ambitious types found in secular employment, and says that hyperactivity has become an endemic disease in Christian circles. He also makes this telling comment:

> Busyness takes over. Driven relentlessly without recognizing the symptoms, we become infected by the disease of activism. It is easy to hide barrenness behind a charade of busyness. To rely on activity, plans, and strategies to cover spiritual bankruptcy.

But is there a solution? Ellis calls us back to the contemplative tradition and the 'waiting on God' that is at the heart of Christianity. He quotes Archbishop Michael Ramsey's reminder that St Dominic's great description of the Christian way was *'Contemplare et contemplata aliis tradere'* (to contemplate and pass on to others the things contemplated). Ramsey asked, 'Is our weakness in the second due to our being often too busy for the first?'

Bob's experience is typical of that of many in Christian leadership. An exceptionally gifted individual, Bob is the international director of a mission agency working in Africa. His job demands a great deal of travel, a huge amount of public speaking, and endless committees and councils. He threw himself wholeheartedly into his work and into leading the mission through a process of change

---

[12] David Ellis, 'Why we may need to do less for God', in *East Asia Millions*, Jan–Mar 1998.

and transition to become more relevant to the twenty-first century. He worked long hours and gave himself unstintingly. Eventually, though, the pace of his life and the demands upon him took their toll. Bob began to show all the classic signs of burnout.

In order to recover, Bob was forced to take time off work. His doctor recommended medication, and a reordering of his lifestyle. Bob himself began to rediscover the grace of God in the midst of his weakness, and to realise that God loved him as much in his inactivity as in his busyness. It helped him to relax more and to slow down. Bob is back at work now, and while the pressures are just as great, his priorities are different. He is learning to look after himself more, has a support group to curb his proneness to over-commit himself, and is giving more time to his relationship with God and the rhythms of grace in his own life.

Bob's story could be repeated countless times. It is the story of too many Christian workers and church leaders. It is an issue we need to address. Evangelical activity and charismatic dynamism need the balance of contemplative stillness if we are to avoid further casualties. We may need not only to do less for God, but also to do things differently. If not, we may well end up burned out on religion.

FOR REFLECTION

1. Do you recognise in yourself a tendency to prefer doing to being? If so, what might be the roots of this?
2. Recall the negative effects of evangelical activism and charismatic dynamism that have been mentioned. Do you see any at work in your own life? If you notice any, think of ways to change things.
3. What can you do to maintain balance in your own life?

Learn from Me

What is the Spirit saying to the church at this time? Could it be that he is calling us to a greater balance in the way we live and minister?

By looking at certain key biblical passages, and in particular the example and teaching of Jesus, we begin to see the need for a more balanced life – one that integrates the strengths of the contemplative tradition with a life of busy servanthood.

At One with God

From rushing around
to stillness,
Lord I come.

From being pulled in all directions
to the simplicity of this moment,
Lord I come.
Help me to realign my will with your will
and my spirit with your Spirit,
as I reach out to you
in the silence.

You are my beloved child.
I will always welcome you
into the rhythm and breath of my life.
Abide in me, and I in you.
Let me love you again into becoming
the person I created you to be.

Angela Ashwin

4

The Example of Jesus

Was Jesus an activist? That is the picture we often have of him from a simple reading of the Gospels. His life was so full and so busy. Crowds demanding his attention, individuals wanting his help. Always on the move, every day packed with incident and controversy. Preaching the kingdom, healing the sick, answering questions. Surrounded by people, bombarded with noise, constantly under pressure. Travelling from place to place, never any privacy, nowhere really to call home. Seldom a moment to himself and certainly no time even to relax.

But was this really the way he lived his life? A closer examination reveals that Jesus was far more balanced in the way he handled himself and managed his time. Reading the gospel story more carefully shows that Jesus was never in a hurry, and always calm in his spirit. Far from being pressurised by the demands upon him, he seems to have made a habit of withdrawing from the hurly-burly in order to be alone with his Father. These interludes of 'aloneness' were integral to the way he lived, and crucial to the maintenance of his relationship with the Father.

It is worth pointing out that Jesus was in no rush to begin

his ministry. From his boyhood adventure in the Temple, to the beginning of his active ministry, we have a long period of silence, of hiddenness. His active ministry lasted only three years. Most of his life was spent in quiet obscurity, growing up in Nazareth, learning about himself and his ministry in the quiet Galilean backwater. It is worth noting too that when he revealed himself publicly at his baptism, the Father showed his approval of his Son: 'You are my Son, whom I love; with you I am well pleased.' (Mark 1:11). This was before ever he had done anything to merit or earn such affirmation.

When eventually his ministry did get under way, it began with a Spirit-led period in the desert. We often assume that this was a negative period of spiritual conflict and hostility, but it seems probable that the temptations came at the end of this period in the desert (Matthew 4:2 says it was *after* 40 days that he was hungry and the temptations began). So why did the Spirit lead Jesus into the wilderness? Presumably so he could be alone with the Father and prepare himself for the ministry that lay ahead. Far from being a negative experience, this period was designed by the Spirit to be a positive time of being built up, of being made ready for the challenges that faced him. Thus we read that Jesus 'returned to Galilee in the power of the Spirit' (Luke 4:14).

During the hectic period of ministry that followed, we can see Jesus carefully maintaining his relationship with the Father through times of strategic withdrawal. Even Mark's breathtaking account of those three years reveals this pattern: 'Very early in the morning, while it was still dark, Jesus got up, left the house and went off to a solitary place, where he prayed' (Mark 1:35). Despite the fact that everyone was looking for him, Jesus disciplined himself to be alone. This didn't happen without considerable cost and inconvenience, or without planning and forethought, but it was such a vital ingredient in his own inner life that he could not manage without it.

We see this same resolve at other times in his life. Luke regards it as part of a behaviour pattern:

> Yet the news about him spread all the more, so that crowds of people came to hear him and to be healed of their sicknesses. But Jesus often withdrew to lonely places and prayed. (Luke 5:15–16)

At crucial times in his ministry he would retire to be alone; for example, before choosing the apostles (Luke 6:12), after John the Baptist died (Matthew 14:13) and before the transfiguration (Matthew 17:1). More importantly, he sought time and space alone in the everyday demands of life, often walking by the lakeside (Mark 2:13; 3:7), or withdrawing to the mountains (Mark 3:13; 6:46; 9:2) and the countryside (John 3:22). Walking through the fields as they journeyed from town to town provided quieter moments, and often when the demands were great, a trip to the other side of the lake gave much needed time alone (Matthew 8:18; 14:13). There were 'safe houses' that he could escape to (Mark 7:24), and friends like the trio at Bethany (Luke 10:38).

Jesus did not avoid the crowds that demanded his attention. Neither did he neglect his responsibilities. But he did guard enough of his time so that he could maintain a living fellowship with his Father:

> His disciples discovered that this regular withdrawal from people and activity was the one predictable thing about Jesus. He made silence and solitude his special companions.

Whatever the demands upon him, he always found a time and space to hide away and be alone.[1]

So why was this kind of strategic withdrawal so important for Jesus? First, because he was human. Like anyone else, Jesus became tired with the constant demands of people, and drained by the pressures of ministry. Being alone was a way of recharging himself, of nourishing his own spirit so that he could continue to give out to others. Time for oneself is a basic human need, and to deny it or neglect it can lead to emotional, spiritual and physical breakdown.

This need for space is not just a matter of personality or temperament. It is true that some people have a preference for being alone (introverts), while others actually derive stimulation and energy from doing things and being with people (extroverts). All of us, however, need time simply to be, when our spirits and souls can be recharged and refreshed. Introverts with busy jobs and lifestyles must ensure that they get sufficient time alone, and not feel guilty when they feel the need to withdraw from the hustle and bustle. Extroverts, because they get a buzz from activity, must be aware of their tendency to run on empty and make sure that they discipline themselves to have quiet spells when they can replenish their inner resources.

A second reason that Jesus withdrew so often was because this was the way in which he maintained his relationship with the Father. He was alone not simply for peace and quiet, but to commune with God: 'In those lonely places the deep springs of the Spirit's life renewed him, the Father's will strengthened him and the Father's love

---

[1] David Runcorn, *Space for God* (Daybreak, 1990), p. 4.

inspired him.'[2] There in the stillness and silence he could hear God speak to him, and there it was he discovered the Father's will for his life. This, of course, was the secret of his ministry.

> 'I tell you the truth, the Son can do nothing by himself; he can do only what he sees his Father doing, because whatever the Father does the Son also does. For the Father loves the Son and shows him all he does . . . By myself I can do nothing; I judge only as I hear, and my judgment is just, for I seek not to please myself but him who sent me.' (John 5:19–20, 30)

It was this secret place of communion with the Father that Jesus guarded so jealously. Since he was dependent on the Father to show him what to say and do, Jesus needed to stay in a place of intimacy, of close contact, of abiding. Out of this deep, inner relationship flowed his life of fruitful ministry. No amount of busyness was allowed to rob him of this place of oneness with the Father, even if the demands were legitimate. His life was punctuated by a deliberate stopping of external activity in order to concentrate on the inner life of the spirit.

> Punctuation is a helpful way of thinking about Jesus' relationship with silence and solitude . . . His times alone were the commas, pauses and full stops in the story of life. They gave the rest of his life its structure, direction and balance. His words and his works were born out of those hours of silent waiting upon God.[3]

The implications of all this for ourselves are obvious. If Jesus needed to take time to be alone and find quietness for

---

[2] David Runcorn, *Space for God* (Daybreak, 1990), p. 4.

[3] *Ibid.*, p. 5.

prayer, then so do we. If the secret of his effectiveness lay in maintaining a place of intimacy and communion with the Father, then that will be the way for us also.

It will not happen automatically or without discipline on our part. We will need to value quietness far more than we do, and to understand the importance of aloneness in developing our walk with God. It will require a change of mindset – from one that simply puts activity first, to one that knows activity must flow out of relationship with the Father. Such a change, however, will bring enormous rewards. Not only a healthier lifestyle, but also a greater clarity in hearing the voice of God.

Jesus has given us an example so that we can follow in his steps. As we consider carefully how he lived, and watch him in action, the Spirit calls us to imitate the Saviour and to ensure a similar balance in our own lives.

FOR REFLECTION

1. What are the benefits of 'strategic withdrawal' as we see them in the life of Jesus?
2. For Jesus, time alone with God was part of his behaviour pattern. As you think about your own lifestyle, how does it help or hinder your walk with God? Is there anything you would like to change?
3. Are you aware of your own humanity and your own legitimate need for space? How do you make provision for it? How do you replenish your inner resources?
4. Where could you create your own special place for communion with God?

5

Come Apart and Be with Me

Not only did Jesus follow a pattern of strategic withdrawal in his own life, he encouraged it in the lives of his followers. They could see for themselves by his example that this was a priority for him. Jesus, however, took it further by actively calling them to experience silence and solitude for themselves.

The occasion came early on in the ministry of Jesus, but already the crowds were gathering and the momentum was beginning. The disciples had been sent out by Jesus two by two for their first taste of ministry, and had returned buoyed up by their success. At the same time, news had just been received of the death of John the Baptist. Probably because of his own need to get away at such an emotional time, and also because it was a crucial time to teach his disciples a foundational lesson, Jesus called them to join in a strategic withdrawal. The full account is given in Mark 6:30–32.

To those newly involved in ministry, busyness is a welcome pressure. It gives the feeling of being effective, of being used by God, of being successful. It creates a good impression too in the eyes of other people. The disciples were certainly busy. They had much to say about what they had already done on their recent ministry trip. Now they were in constant demand from many different quarters, with people coming and going all day long. So busy were they that they had no time even to eat. There was a buzz about the place, and the disciples were loving it!

To their surprise, Jesus calls them to drop everything and follow him to the desert. It must have been puzzling to the disciples to be told to 'down tools' just as things were beginning to happen! Jesus, however, has a different agenda and something important to teach them if they are to be successful in ministry over the long term. Already he can see a worrying trend in what they are doing. This is the second time they have been unable to eat (see Mark 3:20), and a workaholic, needs-driven type of ministry is not the kind of ministry he either models or approves. It is time for them to learn the lesson of a balanced lifestyle. Driven on by their own success, and facing the unrelenting needs of people, the disciples will soon wear themselves out unless they learn how to care for themselves.

'Come with me,' says Jesus. The call to discipleship is first and foremost a call to be in fellowship and friendship with Jesus. How easy it is to let the demands of ministry squeeze out those times of closeness with Jesus. We end up working *for* him rather than being *with* him. When he had first called the disciples, the priority had been clear: first to be with him, and second to be sent out by him (see Mark 3:14). That order was in danger of being reversed, to the detriment of the disciples themselves and those whom they sought to help.

'Come by yourselves.' Jesus wants them to be with him. He values them for who they are, not what they do, and desires to enjoy their company. It means they must leave the work behind and separate themselves from other people. Letting go is never easy. The need to be needed is very great and deeply motivational. Success, once achieved, is not something we easily risk losing. It can seem more prudent to work than to rest.

'To a quiet place.' Quite literally, Jesus invites them into a desert place. Not to what they would immediately regard as a beautiful place, or even an interesting place, but to them a very lonely place. Remote, isolated, solitary, barren. There it is that, free from distractions (even the distractions of legitimate work and deserving people), together they can learn how to spend time in God's presence and hear his still, small voice.

'And get some rest.' 'The bow that is never unstrung will quickly break,' said Chrysostom, echoing the wisdom of Jesus. The Master can see the need for his disciples to build into their hectic schedules periods of rest and refreshment. He calls for a divinely sanctioned intermission. The word used here (*anapauo*) means to cause to rest (body), to soothe (soul), to refresh (spirit). It gives the sense of being renewed in every area of one's being. This is the real rest that Jesus wants to give to all (Matthew 11:29). How important, then, that his representatives are living in the good of it themselves. Worn out, weary and exhausted believers are not a good recommendation for the gospel of rest!

'So they went away by themselves in a boat to a solitary place.' How thankful Jesus must have been for that boat! Time and again we read in the Gospels how he got into the boat and they rowed to the other side of the lake. It was his way of finding peace and quiet, his means of escape. The disciples, whether willingly or not, follow him. They were not always quick to learn, and the lesson that communion with God precedes service for God has never been an easy one for any generation to grasp.

That which Jesus sought to build into the lives of the first apostles is sometimes resisted today. The idea of withdrawal, even strategic withdrawal, seems too defensive for some and defeatist to others. It is, however, part of a balanced and healthy spiritual life. If we are to breathe out, we must first breathe in. There is a natural rhythm to living the Christian life, which William Barclay notes in his commentary on this passage:

> Here we see what might be called the rhythm of the Christian life. For the Christian life is a continuous going into the presence of God from the presence of men, and coming into the presence of men from the presence of God. It is like the rhythm of work and sleep.[1]

Barclay goes on to point out that there are two dangers in life. The first is that of too much activity. The second is that of too much withdrawal. Then he suggests the proper balance with these words: 'The rhythm of the Christian life is the alternate meeting with God in the secret place and serving man in the market place.'[2]

Barclay is right when he emphasises the need for balance. We need both engagement and withdrawal. The danger of modern Christianity, however, is that there is an overemphasis on activity. As we see Jesus teaching his disciples to value the quiet life, we again hear the Spirit calling us to take time to be with the Master.

---

[1] William Barclay, *The Gospel of Mark* (St Andrews Press, 1954), p. 156.
[2] *Ibid.*, p. 156–7.

It may well be that the whole trouble in our lives is that we give God no opportunity to speak to us, because we do not know how to be still and to listen; we give God no time to recharge us with spiritual energy and strength, because there is no time when we wait upon him. How can we shoulder life's burdens if we have no contact with him who is the Lord of all good life? How can we do God's work unless in God's strength? And how can we receive that strength unless we seek, in quietness and in loneliness, the presence of God?[3]

FOR REFLECTION

1. What motivates your Christian service? For instance, do you have a need to be needed? Think carefully about this so that you are not driven in your ministry. What other things motivate you? Are they helpful or not?

2. How do you relax? What are your leisure activities? How are you caring for your body? Your soul? Your spirit? Remember, these are legitimate needs, which God wants you to meet.

3. How can you establish a healthy rhythm of taking in and giving out?

[3] William Barclay, *The Gospel of Mark* (St Andrews Press, 1954), p. 156–7.

6

Learning to Sit

A striking illustration of the importance Jesus gave to the contemplative dimension occurs during one of his frequent visits to the home of his good friends, Mary and Martha. Their home in Bethany was undoubtedly one of the 'safe houses' where Jesus found a haven from the increasing demands of public ministry. However, it was not always an oasis of peace and quiet, as the story described in Luke 10:38–42 reveals.

Perhaps on this occasion Jesus and his disciples arrived unexpectedly and unannounced. Martha, always keen to welcome her guests and look after them properly, is thrown into a panic, and begins hurriedly making preparations in the kitchen. Mary, on the other hand, less flappable than her sister, chooses to sit at the feet of Jesus and listen to what he has to share. It is not long before Martha's sense of injustice boils over into outrage. She has been left (again?) to do all the work, and she feels wronged by her sister. Indignantly, she appeals to Jesus to tell Mary to help her.

We may well feel a great deal of sympathy for Martha. She has a fair point, and we expect Jesus to adjudicate in her favour. But no, to our surprise he takes Mary's side!

70

Mary is the one who has made the right choice. To sit and listen to what the Master has to say is what counts. Martha, with all her customary busyness and desire to please, has allowed herself to be distracted. She has actually missed the main point. This particular guest is not so concerned with being served as with being listened to. It is Martha's attention he wants, not her activity.

What appears to be an ordinary domestic dispute has actually a much profounder significance. It is really about two different approaches to the Christian life. Martha represents the life of busy servanthood, while Mary typifies the life of quiet contemplation. Both are important, but one must have priority. According to Jesus, sitting and listening to what he has to say must come before dashing around in service.

The evangelical and charismatic sections of the church have largely adopted Martha's pattern of busy servanthood. This approach to Christian living is characterised by activity and doing, by serving, caring and helping. It expresses itself through meetings and committees, through projects, programmes and initiatives. It is summed up in visions and goals, and measured in objectives and achievements. It requires a great deal of effort, and those who live this way must be highly committed.

The life of quiet contemplation is very different. It is about being rather than doing, about becoming rather than achieving. It expresses itself through reflection, meditation and contemplation. It requires quietness and stillness, time and space, solitude and silence. It is about listening rather than talking, resting rather than working. It is about letting God be God, and waiting for him to act.

The life of busy servanthood has of course good biblical precedent. Just prior to this incident, Jesus had told the parable of the Good Samaritan, which ends with a challenge to 'go and do likewise' (Luke 10:37). Many of us have heard those words, and ever since have been going and doing. Unfortunately, we have not always heard the other words, which call us to sit and listen. We have become distracted and we have neglected our fellowship with Jesus.

As we have seen earlier, evangelical/charismatic spirituality values busyness. We are often asked, 'Are you busy?' and like to be able to answer, 'Yes, very!' Busyness makes us feel good. It gives us the impression we are achieving something; that we are going somewhere. We may of course be achieving very little, and going round in circles, but at least we are doing something! Churches that are 'alive' have busy programmes, and 'active' Christians are involved in everything! So it is that we get trapped in a self-perpetuating cycle of busyness.

The result is that there is an increasing number of highly committed Christians stressed out by trying to balance the demands of home and work and church. Luke the physician accurately diagnoses Martha's 'hurry sickness'[1]. She is 'distracted' (literally, wheeling about, overbusied), 'worried' (literally, anxious and careworn) and 'upset' (literally, troubled, disturbed, in a state of mental agitation). Not a pretty picture, but sadly an accurate description of many in the contemporary church, especially the leaders!

---

[1] A phrase coined by James Gleick in his book *Faster – the Acceleration of just about Everything* (Vintage Books, 1999). He describes the ever-increasing pace of life in society and the effect that has on people as they desperately try to keep up. By and large the church allows itself to be caught up in the same rush to do more things more quickly. Rather than modelling a different lifestyle, we are carried along on the same tide of ceaseless activity.

What is needed is a rediscovery of contemplative spirituality, a return to the practice of sitting at the feet of Jesus. But what is required for this to happen? First, we will need to stop. For those addicted to a busy lifestyle this may be a frightening thought, but it is essential that we learn the discipline of stopping. We need to take time out of busy schedules to be quiet and alone with God. We need enough time to switch off from the daily demands and to switch on to God again. We must rediscover the values of daily times alone with God, of quiet days and retreats.

Second, we will need to sit. We need to learn how to rest without feeling guilty, and to rest not just physically, but inwardly too. We need to find that sabbath rest that still awaits the people of God – a rest that comes from letting God take the strain in our lives and ministries. It is God's work after all, and the responsibility rightly belongs on his shoulders. To enter God's rest we must cease from our own labours. Only when we are truly at rest can we receive the revelation that we need to work effectively.

Third, we will need to listen. When our hearts are quiet, and the noise of our own activity has ceased, we will again hear the voice of God. His word is life and light. When he speaks, we know what we should be doing. Work commissioned by God carries its own blessing and authentication. It is effective. We may indeed end up doing less for God, but what we do will be more fruitful and not so exhausting.

Jesus commended Mary because she had chosen 'the good part'. There is a choice to be made, and what we choose is important. It is not an 'either/or' choice, however, but rather a question of which comes first; what is foundational to our lives. In spiritual terms, work proceeds from a place of rest. Our life of busy servanthood must be underpinned by a life of quiet contemplation. The challenge is to ensure that we give due attention to this part of our lives.

Jesus said of Mary 'It will not be taken from her.' The fruits of contemplation are seen in the transformation of our inner lives, in the formation of character, the shaping of attitudes, the internalising of values. These are lasting benefits. Activity may or may not produce results. Being with Jesus certainly will.

Once more we hear the call of the Spirit. There in the house at Bethany, he beckons us to a greater *intimacy* with the Master. To sit at his feet and listen. This is what the Lord requires.

FOR REFLECTION

1. Which of the sisters do you identify with more easily, and why?
2. What do you think are the symptoms of 'hurry sickness' in our society? Do you recognise any in your own life?
3. Why not try the three simple steps that characterise a contemplative approach?
   - Stop – deliberately plan some time out from your schedule.
   - Sit – find a comfortable place to be quiet, and relax yourself.
   - Listen – tune in to God. What does he say to you?

7

Bearing Fruit the Easy Way

For several years I had a poster in my office with a picture of St George slaying the dragon. Underneath were these words: 'What will you be remembered for?'

It is an important question. We all know what St George is remembered for, but what kind of legacy will we leave behind? What will people say about us when our life is over? What impact will we have made on the world?

Christians above all should be concerned to make their lives count, to live 'on purpose' in Tom Sine's telling phrase. Part of that purpose is clearly that we should give our lives to serving God, to sharing in his eternal purpose for the world. It is to this that many of us have given ourselves energetically and enthusiastically; doing our utmost for his highest, as Oswald Chambers would say. We have done so gladly and willingly, for this is part of what it means to be a disciple and follower of Jesus: 'You did not choose me, but I chose you and appointed you to go and bear fruit – fruit that will last' (John 15:16).

I can still remember clearly the day when as a 15-year-old boy I became conscious for the first time that God was calling me to himself. There in the tiny Methodist chapel in the village where I had grown up, God broke into my life. Almost immediately I knew as well that he wanted me to serve him. It seemed to be part of the deal. I wasn't sure exactly how I would serve him, but I knew I had to give my whole life to him, and that he had a plan and purpose for my life.

Jesus made it clear that God wants our lives to bear fruit for him. If we are truly his disciples, there will be some tangible expression of service in our lives: 'This is to my Father's glory, that you bear much fruit, showing yourselves to be my disciples' (John 15:8). So it is that any believer who takes seriously the claims of Christ on their life will be involved in some form of Christian service. It is both the Father's wish and the disciple's desire, and most of us set about the task of living for Jesus with an abundance of zeal and determination.

It is just here that the problem lies. First, we often throw ourselves into Christian ministry with our own human zeal and natural energy. It sometimes takes many tiring years of effort, and lots of painful failures, before we finally come to an end of ourselves and begin to learn one of the most important spiritual lessons of all – that apart from Christ we can do nothing (John 15:5).

More than that, though, our very focus on doing things for God gets in the way of what ought to be a priority for us, and which is anyway the secret of fruitfulness in ministry: our relationship with him. What so often happens is that we become so immersed in worthwhile activity, so committed to the cause, that we neglect our fellowship with God – the very thing that would ensure our effectiveness.

Jesus was at great pains to instruct his disciples that if they wanted to bear fruit that would stand the test of time they must stay in living contact with himself. He likened it to the way a branch abides in the vine and so bears fruit naturally and easily. The secret of a fruitful life is just as simple: we are to abide in Christ.

> I am the Vine, you are the branches. When you're joined with me and I with you, the relation intimate and organic, the harvest is sure to be abundant. Separated, you can't produce a thing. (John 15:5, *The Message*)

We don't have to work ourselves to the bone or drive ourselves into the dust in order to bear fruit for God. It isn't about doing more, trying harder or redoubling our efforts. The secret lies in being connected to Jesus in a living, vital relationship. In other words, the key to effective service is deeper intimacy, not increased activity.

Bruce Wilkinson is a respected Bible teacher and leader of an international Christian organisation in America. Some 15 years ago he reached a point in his ministry where, although he was outwardly successful, inwardly he was running on empty. His passion for ministry seemed to have gone, and although he was working harder than ever, he had less satisfaction than at any other time in his life. In desperation he went to talk to a respected mentor and friend. Their conversation soon revealed the cause of his problem: he had been neglecting his relationship with God. Painfully the truth dawned on him: 'God didn't want me to do more *for* Him. He wanted me to be more *with* Him.'[1]

The whole experience led Wilkinson to a new appreciation of abiding in Christ, and to a new level of fruitfulness in ministry, which he has since been able to share with

---

[1] Bruce Wilkinson, *Secrets of the Vine* (Multomah, 2002), ch. 7, p. 93.

thousands around the world. He saw that he must make intimacy with God his first priority. He writes:

> His purpose is not that you will do more for Him but that you will choose to be more with Him. Only by abiding can you enjoy the most rewarding friendship with God and experience the greatest abundance for His glory.[2]

Friendship is what it is all about, and we have to make room for that friendship in our busy schedules. If need be we have to trim our lives of distractions and alternatives, however praiseworthy they may be, in order that we can give time to our relationship with Jesus. This then becomes the source of our life, and we begin to live out of our relationship with him. In this way, it is his life that begins to operate in us rather than our own, and we experience what some have called 'the exchanged life', which is Christ living his life through us.

Intimacy, of course, requires the investment of quality time. As Andrew Murray said, 'It takes time to grow into Jesus the Vine; do not expect to abide in Him unless you will give Him that time.'[3] We take time to pray, to worship, to soak up his word, to dwell in his presence, to listen for his voice. We have time to linger, to relax, to be with him without any agenda, to enjoy him without making any demands. We will look later at practical ways by which we can abide, but we must always remember that abiding is about being with a person, not mastering a formula or technique. Steve McVey puts it very clearly when he says:

---

[2] Bruce Wilkinson, *Secrets of the Vine* (Multomah, 2002), p. 96.
[3] Andrew Murray, *Abide in Christ* (Nisbet), p. 7.

Abiding in Christ isn't achieved by successfully following certain steps. It's an act of faith by which we simply choose to believe that He is our life, that He will express Himself through us, and then act as if He is doing that very thing at this very moment. Abundant living isn't found in a plan, but in the Person of Jesus Christ. That fact can't be overstated or emphasised too many times.[4]

If you want to learn to abide in Christ, don't worry about the right or wrong way to do it. Simply make it your aim to be with Jesus and enjoy his friendship, and the rest will take care of itself. Come into his presence and dwell in his love (John 15:9), make yourself at home in his acceptance of you, and allow yourself to be filled again with his life. This is the essence of abiding.

We have seen already that Jesus was effective in ministry because he took time to abide in his Father's love, continually escaping from the pressures and demands in order to be renewed and refreshed by time alone with God (see Chapter 4). As we watch him at work we learn how to work with him. His example becomes our pattern. If it worked for him, it will work for us. As we learn to abide we will discern more clearly exactly what it is God wants us to do. So much of our work is ineffective because it is uncommanded work – a good idea on our part rather than a God idea originating in him. It is as we wait on God that we are better able to hear what God is saying and become more attentive to his voice. We begin to recognise more readily the Spirit's promptings, and are more responsive to his leading. Then our only concern is to obey. If we are hearing God's voice and doing his will it is certain to be fruitful.

---

[4] Steve McVey, *The Divine Invitation* (Harvest House, 2002), p. 134.

Not only that, but as we dwell in his presence we are energised by the Spirit and strengthened for the task. Rather than being constantly drained because we are working in our own energy, we learn how to operate out of the strength of Christ within us. We discover the 'rest' of God, that relaxedness that enhances everything we do. Rather than being uptight and on edge (the mark of human effort), we are relaxed and natural in what we do (the mark of God at work in us). Thus we work both more efficiently and more effectively. By doing less we may actually end up doing more!

The branch takes no credit for producing fruit. It is the life of the vine that does that. Its only responsibility is to stay joined to the vine, and then fruit-bearing is natural and easy. Likewise, if we desire to bear fruit for God, our only responsibility is to stay in union with Christ and respond to the movement of his life within us. Thus we can live freely and lightly, bearing fruit the easy way.

FOR REFLECTION

1. What would you say is the purpose of your life? How does it fit into God's plan for your life?
2. What do you understand now by 'abiding in Christ'? How could you ensure that you do not miss out on your relationship with God?
3. What do you think the 'exchanged life' is all about? How might it be relevant to you?

8

Centred on Jesus

'Eccentric.' Few of us would appreciate such a description, but eccentric is what many of us are. The word means to be off-centre, and when it comes to the way we live our lives, a good number of us could justifiably be described as being off-centre. For while the Christian life is meant to be lived with Jesus at the centre, our busyness and focus on activity has often relegated him to the circumference of our lives.

Michael Frye's compelling song 'Jesus be the Centre' has resonated with many people simply because they recognise they are living eccentrically.[1] They long instinctively for Jesus to be the source of their life; their hope, their guide. They want him to be the wind in their sails, the fire in their hearts and the reason they live. This modern-day psalm expresses exactly the anguished cry of many contemporary children of God. They yearn to put Jesus back at the centre of life.

The writer to the Hebrews shared a similar sentiment. His letter is written with the aim of encouraging first-century believers to keep on believing despite the pressures.

---

[1] Michael Frye, 'Be the Centre', Vineyard Songs, 1999 (UK/Eire). Available on the CD *Hungry*, Vineyard Music.

They are in danger of drifting away, of letting go of their grip, of throwing away their confidence. He is concerned lest they become discouraged and neglect their salvation. Some have already stopped meeting for fellowship; others are getting tangled up in sin again. Most disconcertingly, they have begun to lose their focus on Jesus. They too are becoming eccentric.

Into this context the writer speaks with clarity and conviction about the centrality of Jesus. He calls them back to a Christ-centred faith: 'Let us fix our eyes on Jesus,' he urges (Hebrews 12:1–3). Whatever the pressures, whatever the distraction, this is the answer: take another look at Jesus, fix your gaze upon him and become engrossed with him once again. Such a preoccupation is more than adequate to cure the malady of soul that has overtaken them. The answer to the pull of sin is not greater discipline, stricter rules or trying harder. It is to fall in love with Jesus all over again. The person who is besotted with him has no difficulty in casting sin aside.

Athletic contests were popular throughout the ancient world. Using imagery extremely familiar to his readers, the writer to the Hebrews likens the Christian life to a race, and these are runners who have become exhausted. They are in danger of collapsing long before the finishing line. They need to be refreshed and reinvigorated, otherwise they will not make it. He says they are weary and about to lose heart – a description that aptly summarises the way many in church feel today.

'Weary' translates a word which means to tire with exertion, to labour to weariness, to feel exhausted, to become sick. The second expression, 'to lose heart', is literally 'fainting in the souls of you', suggesting despondency, a condition of being mentally weary, of having nothing left

to give, of having lost all creativity. Today we would call
this burnout, and the symptoms are all too familiar to those
of us who have pastoral care of church leaders, missionaries and people who work in Christian organisations. If we
are to recover our lives, we will need to come to Jesus and
learn from him. We will need to fix our eyes once more
upon him.

The writer to the Hebrews calls his readers to consider
Jesus (12:3), just as he had earlier encouraged them to 'fix
their thoughts on Jesus' (3:1). Again, the word he uses is of
interest. 'To consider' means to look carefully at, to gaze
upon, to look with loving attentiveness. It is a word sometimes used of astronomers, who gaze at the heavens with
diligence and concentration. It reminds me of a young man
I read about in the south-west of England who was watching the stars one night through his home-made telescope.
Such was the intensity and carefulness of his gaze that he
saw a star that had never been seen before. His discovery
was verified and he was given the honour of naming the
newly identified star. What concentration! What dedication
to star-gazing! If we are to shake off our spiritual lethargy
and cure our spiritual exhaustion, what are we to do?
Nothing, except look lovingly and adoringly at Jesus. We
are to turn our eyes upon him, deliberately and definitely
making him the centre of our attention.

King David in the Old Testament knew the benefit and
blessing of worshipping God and, in the context of worship,
allowing his gaze to rest on the Lord. That is why in Psalm
27 we read that his lifelong prayer was: 'One thing I ask of
the Lord, this is what I seek: that I may dwell in the house
of the Lord all the days of my life, to gaze upon the beauty
of the Lord and to seek him in his temple' (v.4). This warrior
king, this man after God's own heart, had only one real

desire. He longed to know God more intimately, to be more at home in his presence, to appreciate more fully his beauty.

This is the only biblical reference to the beauty of the Lord (though there are many to his glory). It is an unusual expression, the language of love and devotion rather than of theology and doctrine. We are more accustomed to speaking about the attributes of God, and to analysing his qualities and systematising his activities, than to feeling his attractiveness and desirability. 'Beauty' takes us into another realm altogether – the subjective, affective realm where emotions and feelings are real and valued.

'The beauty of the Lord' is an attempt to describe the overall impact or impression that the Lord in his complete-ness makes upon those who encounter him. It tries to sum up the feelings generated by the totality of who God is. When we meet God in the person of Jesus we experience beauty – sheer loveliness, tenderness, compassion, charm and grace. Words are inadequate to convey what is felt, what is known intuitively. Once we have experienced it, however, we are refreshed, renewed, revitalised. We thirst for more of him, and we do so with the assurance that if we seek him, we shall find him; if we have a longing for him, it will eventually be satisfied.

David and the godly men and women in the Old Testament knew what it was to wait on God. They knew how to linger in his presence and how to seek his face in quiet, contemplative prayer. They knew themselves to be dependent upon God, and they were content to wait for God to reveal himself; to wait for him to act in his own chosen time. They were not hurried or rushed in his pres-ence. They had time to 'waste', time to pour out on the God whom they adored. There, in the secret place, they discov-ered true rest: 'Find rest, O my soul, in God alone; my hope comes from him. He alone is my rock and my salvation; he is my fortress, I shall not be shaken' (Psalm 62:5–6).

This fixing our eyes upon Jesus that the writer of Hebrews calls for involves the same contemplative approach. We are to allow the Spirit to make Jesus real to us, and through our worship, prayer and meditation allow ourselves to be recentred. He takes the fragmented pieces of our lives and puts them back together again. Looking to Jesus helps to reintegrate us. As we wait on the Lord, we find that our strength is renewed. We are able to mount up like eagles, carried on the currents of divine love and grace, held aloft by the sustaining wind of the Spirit. Then it is that we are empowered to run and not grow weary, to walk and never faint (see Isaiah 40:27–31).

Our attention is to be fully upon Jesus, and if we have been distracted by busyness, or side-tracked by secondary issues, we are to consciously focus on him. We are to concentrate on who he is: the author and the perfecter of our faith. He is the one who began this good work in us, and that is the guarantee that he will bring it to completion (see Philippians 1:6). We can depend upon the working of his mighty power within us. He is also committed to sustaining us and to strengthening our faith along the way, so we need not fear falling by the wayside. Tired and weary as we are, we dare to rest in him, for he is the one who brought us to God in the first place, and he is the one who will carry us through.

As we allow our eyes to return to him we look once more to the cross and are reminded of all he has done for us there. We allow our minds to be filled again with the wonder of everything his saving death has accomplished for us. He has taken away our sins completely and for all time. We have been reconciled to the Father, totally forgiven of all our sins (past, present and future) and brought back into a permanent love relationship with him. As we meditate on these foundational truths, the sheer joy and delight of who we are in Christ, and all that is ours in him, can begin to flood our hearts and minds again. Our souls are restored, our faith is refreshed, our hope is rekindled.

More than that, as we gaze upon him we notice where he is: seated at God's right hand, enthroned in heaven. He is the one who died, but who rose again, and now has ascended victoriously. From this place of rule and authority he is now able to pour his grace into our lives moment by moment and day by day (Hebrews 4:14–16). Fortified by this gift of divine strength we are more able to cope with the pressures and trials of life. Strangely, this infusion of grace comes about when we give up our own futile struggle to overcome by our own efforts, and instead do nothing but wait upon God. It is almost as if God were waiting for us to come to an end of ourselves in order that his divine life might take over. He does not ask us to do more, but simply to look in faith towards him.

Here again we see the wonder of divine grace and the invitation to intimacy. It is not offered to the deserving as a reward for successful living, but to the needy to sustain them in their weakness. That is why we need not fear to draw near. We will not be rejected or shut out. We will meet with mercy, not judgement; with acceptance, not condemnation. We can come just as we are and find grace to help us in our time of need.

At this point the contemplative dimension moves us back into the activist realm, for there is a race to be run, and there is a course marked out for each of us. Looking to Jesus provides us with the inspiration to run the race. The contemplative is again seen to be the bedrock of the practical. This race is no saunter along country lanes, either, but a vigorous marathon that takes us through rough and rugged terrain. The road ahead of us has its ups and downs, its twists and turns. It is both exhilarating and dangerous. Many surprises await us; many challenges will meet us on the way. We need stamina, determination and guts – all that the writer means by perseverance (12:1). To do the will of God in the world today is not easy, for it takes us to the hardest of places and the neediest of people. There is often opposition, always temptation. We will be stretched to the limit if we follow Jesus, but never overwhelmed if our eyes remain fixed on him.

The key to running well and to finishing the course lies in our being centred on him. As Andrew Murray puts it:

> Looking to Jesus, with the look of faith, because salvation is in Him alone;
> with the look of love, because He alone can satisfy the heart;
> with the look of strong desire, longing to know Him better;
> with the look of soul devotion, waiting only to know His will;
> with the look of gladness, because we know He loves us;
> with the look of wonder and admiration, for He is the brightness of the Father's glory, our Lord and our God.[2]

Whatever our calling, and wherever it takes us, we can do no better than this.

FOR REFLECTION

1. Imagine a circle with Jesus at the centre. Where would you place yourself in relation to him?

---

[2] Andrew Murray, *The Holiest of All* (Marshall, Morgan & Scott, 1960), p. 484.

2. If you find yourself to be off-centre, why might that be? Because of entanglements? Distractions? Exhaustion? Something else?

3. How can you fix your eyes upon Jesus again and become recentred? Remember his grace waits only to welcome you, not to condemn you.

Get Away with Me

The invitation to intimacy that Jesus gives us inevitably involves a call to be alone with him. The pressures of life do not make this easy to do, and neither does the ethos of contemporary evangelical and charismatic Christianity, obsessed as it is with activity and achievement. However, we are recognising increasingly the need for a greater balance in the way we live the Christian life. Those of us who are busy activists need to build into our lives more time and space for God. If we are to do this, we must learn how to be still, and then how to listen quietly to God. While we may be able to do this in the company of others, it will be better achieved through times of being alone. Stillness, silence and solitude are the basic ingredients of contemplative spirituality, and it is to an examination of these factors that we now turn. While they belong together and overlap with each other, for the sake of clarity we will look at each in turn.

Simply Being

Quiet prayer is a matter of being:
Being in stillness,
Being in God;
Not to achieve anything
Or trying to find words,
But simply being.

I am here, Lord,
Hiding nothing from you,
Holding back nothing from you;
I simply wait in your presence.
For when I wait for you
I am found by you.

Angela Ashwin

9

Stillness

I remember reading to my children a very popular book called *Richard Scary's Busy, Busy World*. Every colourful page was a mass of detail, with all kinds of people doing all kinds of things. The children pored over each page, eager to see what the various characters were doing. So much was happening in every illustration! They were fascinated by the variety, and never tired of talking about what they saw. Without realising it, of course, I was introducing them to the idea that the world is a very busy place, and that everyone who lives there ought to be busy too!

We cannot isolate ourselves from the demands of daily living. The world is a busy place, and it is getting busier all the time. Rather than creating more leisure, technology has increased the pace of life. Quicker transportation and faster communication in particular have speeded things up so that we are expected to do more, and in a shorter space of time. Inevitably we become caught up in the whirl of activity and movement that surrounds us, and find ourselves living to the beat and rhythm of a society that is increasingly wound up. In such a context it is extremely difficult to slow down and adopt a gentler tempo.

We have our own internal pressures too. The hustle and bustle are as much within us as outside us. We want to succeed, to make progress, to do well. We have an in-built need to achieve and to prove ourselves. We want to create the right impression and live up to the expectations of others. Christians can be just as competitive as others, and equally as keen to outdo their counterparts (we would not call them rivals). As much as we would like to think that the motivation for our Christian service is entirely pure, in reality we can be moved as much by our need to achieve and to make our mark as by a desire to glorify God.

In such a context, the very idea of slowing down, let alone stopping, becomes threatening and risky. If we let up on our busyness, even for a moment, will we fall behind in the race? If we ease up on our schedules and do less, will we somehow fail to reach our targets? If we are still, how can we achieve? And yet we know that if we are to experience God in a deeper way, we will have to make time and space to be with him. We will need to learn and practise the discipline of stopping.

Ken Blanchard is the author of *The One-Minute Manager* and a leading management consultant. In an article entitled 'Don't work harder – work smarter' he highlights one of the important lessons of leadership:

> Most people mentally have a sign on their desk that reads: Don't just sit there, do something! The best advice I ever received was to redo the sign to read: Don't just do something, sit there![1]

Psalm 46 contains one of the most compelling reasons for learning to be still. God himself is speaking, at a time when

---

[1] *Christianity & Renewal* magazine, February 2001.

society is in turmoil and even the most stable things are giving way. This is his exhortation: 'Be still, and know that I am God' (Psalm 46:10). There are some things about God that can only be known in stillness, and through being quiet in his presence. We can know God to a certain degree, and at a certain level, in the midst of our activity and busyness, but the more intimate knowledge of God is reserved for those who will quieten themselves and be still before him. It is this deeper knowledge of God that will keep us stable through times of turmoil and change, as Psalm 46 indicates.

When we speak here about knowing God, we are talking about what we call revelation knowledge – an awareness that goes beyond the facts we know about God in our heads, and becomes the truth that grips us in our hearts. This kind of revelation, in my experience, usually comes in moments when I am relaxed in God's presence, when I have taken the time to sit and be still, and to wait on God. Then it is that some particular insight will come to me. Stillness seems to be a prerequisite for such revelation. It creates the environment in which our spirit becomes receptive to God and attuned to his Spirit.

This stillness of soul is further described for us in Psalm 131. Here the psalmist approaches God in humility, and deliberately quietens himself before the Lord: 'But I have stilled and quietened my soul; like a weaned child with its mother, like a weaned child is my soul within me' (v.2). Through this tender imagery we can see what is involved in the process of stilling ourselves. We can picture a fractious child, screaming and crying, agitated and distressed. Then comes the succour and comfort of the mother's breast. Gradually the child quietens and becomes content. Instead of wriggling and writhing, the little body stills and is presently asleep.

According to the psalmist, this is something we must learn to do before God. Often we come to him in a state of agitation and distress. We are troubled and anxious. We are wound up inside, coiled like a spring, full of inner tension. Our greatest need is to be able to relax ourselves. But how can we do this? By resting in God's great love for us, by allowing him to succour us. As we consciously still ourselves and begin drawing on the great truths of his mercy and grace, his peace begins to flow into our troubled minds. This doesn't happen instantaneously or automatically. It takes time. It requires us to discipline our mind and our emotions. Gradually, however, a stillness of soul creeps over us, and with it that contentedness which makes it easier for us to 'know' our God.

Outer stillness

For this to happen there has to be an outer stillness. This means that we have to separate ourselves from our work and activity, and from the legitimate demands on our time, even if for a short period. It is not always easy to achieve, but with self-discipline and good planning, it is possible to make time even within the busiest of diaries.

Evangelicals are familiar with the idea of a daily quiet time. Unfortunately, this often has very little 'quiet' within it. Mostly the time is given to Bible reading and intercessory prayer – both worthwhile activities, but activities just the same. With a little adaptation, the framework of a regular quiet time can provide an ideal opportunity for stillness and a silent waiting upon God.

For those who do not follow such a regular pattern, it is important to set aside quality time to be with God, and to practise the discipline of stopping. When I worked at a

Christian conference centre, we had a daily mid-morning time of prayer. It is surprising how strong the temptation was to skip this time, especially when the workload was heavy! It requires a quality decision, and a measure of faith, to stop and spend time with God. We need to plan into our programme non-negotiable time to be with God, recognising its value and importance, and realising that it will not happen by chance or by accident – we will need to make it happen. Even 15 minutes of stillness on a regular basis (daily if possible) can provide an oasis of calm and refreshment in the midst of a busy life.

Graham and Jo are both busy people, but even when their children were small they determined to find a quiet place in the midst of the hurly-burly of family life. They erected a little shed in their garden and used it in turns each morning as a place to escape to from the noise and pressure of their daily lives. It became an oasis for them, and provided the opportunity they needed to find stillness with God in the midst of all their activity.

For some, the taking of a regular quiet day has provided the necessary breathing space in a hectic schedule – perhaps one day a month, or every quarter, reserved in order to get away to a quiet place and be alone with God. The venue, of course, is important. It needs to be a place where one can feel relaxed and be undisturbed. Being surrounded by beautiful countryside is a help, and buildings with a prayerful and peaceful atmosphere make it easier to seek God. Such a day can be taken alone or in the company of others.

Jonathan is the leader of a growing church in the north of England. He is the kind of person who involves himself in everything that is going on around him, and who is always ready to respond to the needs of others. Increasingly he has realised, however, the need to have time and space for himself. Every month now he sets aside in his diary a day for reading and reflection. He travels to a nearby Christian training centre and finds a quiet corner in the library, where he knows he will not be disturbed. It is his way of making sure his life does not become over-busy and that he has quality time with God.

Increasing numbers of people are finding it helpful to go on retreat, and to spend several days away from the normal daily demands in order to be with God and to nurture and develop their inner life. There are a growing number of retreat centres and programmes on offer to meet this need. For some, however, the idea of a retreat sounds a defeatist note. As someone said to me, 'I don't want to retreat, brother. I want to advance!' Perhaps if we think of a retreat as a 'strategic withdrawal' it will make more sense to those for whom it is a difficult term – for essentially that is what it is: an opportunity to withdraw for a while in order to gain a better perspective and to be renewed for the ongoing battle.[2]

Having made space and time for God, we still have to deal with the process of winding down, which may not come at all easily to the more hyperactive! Actually being still physically can be a challenge to someone who is restlessly on the go, and most energetic people find it takes a while to really slow down. A comfortable chair will help, of course, and some basic relaxation techniques. Wanda Nash, an experienced retreat leader, has written helpfully in *Christ, Stress and Glory* about the place of breathing in

---

[2] For a fuller discussion of the value of retreats see John Pearce, *Advance by Retreat – Using Silence to Come Closer to God* (Grove Books, 1989).

helping us to relax.[3] In contemplative terminology this is called 'centring' oneself. She also gives an excellent description of how to spend a short time being still with God.

To put her recommendations simply, it is a matter of learning to breathe more slowly. As we find a place to relax ourselves, such as lying on the floor, we can let our breathing slow down until we begin to breathe automatically, from the belly rather than the chest. As we do this we soon find the body's natural rhythm, which is much slower than what we are used to. Soon the rest of the body comes to stillness, and we find ourselves at peace. This is a good technique to use when sleep is difficult or we are feeling tense about something.

Another technique that has proven value is that of using a rhythm prayer. Here a very simple prayer is repeated over and over again in rhythm with one's breathing. The most well known is the Jesus Prayer, which has been used in this way for centuries. As you breathe in you pray (either silently or out loud), 'Jesus Christ, Son of God,' and then as you breathe out, 'Have mercy on me.' As well as being a very profound prayer, the rhythmic repeating of it has a calming effect. It is recommended that you sit very still, with palms raised towards God in a receptive gesture. These are not magical words, however, and we can substitute other words that are just as scriptural and which meet more appropriately our need at a particular moment, for example 'Spirit of the living God/Fall afresh on me' or 'Father in heaven/Hallowed be your name'.

---

[3] Wanda Nash, *Christ, Stress and Glory* (DLT, 1997). See the section on pp. 27–32 for a helpful explanation of appropriate breathing, and the difference between belly breathing and chest breathing. See pp. 172–7 for helpful practical guidance on how to be still with God.

Inner stillness

If outer stillness is difficult to achieve, then inner stillness can be even more elusive. We may find ourselves sitting quietly in some beautiful setting, but with a great restlessness swirling around inside of us. For evangelicals, it seems important that we are able to give ourselves permission to be still, and this means having good scriptural warrant for being what we might call inactive or off duty. Without this we tend to be plagued by guilt and find it impossible to rest or relax. This is where a proper understanding of the Sabbath principle can come to our aid.

Far from being merely a piece of restrictive legislation, the command to keep a sabbath (Exodus 20:8–11) enshrines a very vital spiritual truth. God worked for six days, and then rested. The call to keep a sabbath was a call to enter into the rest of God; to stop our own activity and focus on God, and to share his satisfaction in a job well done.

Not surprisingly, this call to rest and cease from our own activities, even for one day, meets with great resistance in our modern society. Commerce and business cannot wait; sport and leisure demand our time. Sunday has become a day like any other day, full of busyness and activity. In rejecting the call for a sabbath, we have rejected the need for stillness and rest, and are poorer as a result. Christians have suffered as much as anyone from this by allowing themselves to follow the trends of society, and in their failure to keep a true day of rest.[4]

---

[4] For a wonderful explanation and application of the sabbath principle in relation to modern living see Wayne Muller, *Sabbath Rest* (Lion, 1999) and Marva J. Dawn, *Keeping the Sabbath Wholly* (Eerdmans, 1989). Another helpful book for busy church leaders is Patrick

However, behind the external call for a specific day of rest is a more urgent and pressing call to rest in God. This is the true sabbath, where we allow God his rightful place in our lives and trust him in creaturely dependence to do all for us. It is a difficult lesson to learn, for our nature is to be independent of God and to act out of our own strength and effort to solve our problems and achieve our goals. Stopping our own activities and becoming still is therefore an act of faith in which we express our trust in God to work on our behalf. Richard Foster has written:

> No teaching flowing out of the Sabbath principle is more important than the centrality of our resting in God. Instead of striving to make this or that happen, we learn to trust in a heavenly Father who loves to give. This does not promote inactivity, but it does promote dependent activity. No longer do we take things into our own hands. Rather, we place all things into divine hands and then act out of inner promptings.[5]

This same truth is brought out for us in Hebrews 4, where the writer reminds us that 'the promise of entering his rest still stands' (v.1). He notes that Israel did not enter the Promised Land (where they would have found rest) because of their unbelief and disobedience. However, those who do believe and have faith can still enter into God's Sabbath rest: 'There remains, then, a Sabbath-rest for the people of God; for anyone who enters God's rest also rests from his own work, just as God did from his' (v.9). To rest

Klingamaan, *Finding Rest When the Work Is Never Done* (Cook Communications, 2000).
[5] Richard Foster, *Prayer* (Hodder & Stoughton, 1992). The quotation is from p. 100, in an excellent and very relevant chapter called 'The prayer of rest'. Used by permission of Hodder & Stoughton Ltd.

in this sense means to live in the power of God rather than in our own energy and strength. It means that we depend on God to make things happen. We learn to receive from him all that we need to do his will. We depend upon the prior activity of God in our lives, and then respond in obedience. Andrew Murray, one of the greatest exponents of the inner life, comments on this verse:

> Entering the rest of God is the ceasing from self-effort and the yielding up of oneself in the full surrender of faith to God's working . . . As the Almighty, God is the only source of power. In nature He works all. In grace He waits to work all too, if man will but consent and allow. Truly to rest in God is to yield oneself up to the highest activity.[6]

Just as we love because he first loved us, so we work because he first moves within us. As we wait upon God, we expect him to create within us both the desire and the ability to do his will (Philippians 2:13). We labour, but with all the energy that he inspires within us (Colossians 1:29). Being still before him is therefore an essential part of allowing his Spirit to work in us in this way.

From this perspective, faith gives rest because it rests in God, and will mean ceasing from what has been called 'creaturely activity'; that is, the prideful expression of our independent self.

> Faith is always repose in what Another will do for me. Faith ceases to seek help in itself or its own efforts, to be troubled with its need or its weakness; it rests in the sufficiency of the all-sufficient One who has undertaken all.[7]

---

[6] Andrew Murray, *The Holiest of All* (Revell, 1960), p. 152.
[7] *Ibid.*, p. 146.

For busy activists, being still for a while and letting go of our own activity may seem like a death, which indeed it is – a death to the old independent way of living, in order that the new life of the Spirit may be at work in us.

Resting in God does not mean resignation or idleness. What it does mean is that we are to work *from* a place of rest, not *towards* a place of rest. There is a world of difference between the two. Our ability to stop what we are doing and be still before God is an indicator of which direction our life is moving in, and where the source of our strength really lies.

Watchman Nee, the great Chinese Christian writer, has some helpful insights on this in his commentary on Ephesians. In seeking to explain what it means, that we are seated with Christ (Ephesians 2:6), he points out that after God had made the world in six days, he rested on the seventh. Adam was created on the sixth day, so his first day was a day of rest. He began with a day off!

> Whereas God worked six days and then enjoyed His sabbath rest, Adam began his life with the sabbath; for God works before He rests, while man must first enter into God's rest, and then alone can he work.[8]

According to Nee, this is the principle by which God always works. It was because God had finished his work of creation that Adam could begin by enjoying what God had already done for him. Likewise with our salvation. God has done everything for us in Christ at the cross. We simply step by faith into the enjoyment of his finished work. There is nothing for us to do – indeed we need to give up our own works in order to benefit from his.

---

8 Watchmen Nee, *Sit, Walk, Stand* (Victory Press, 1957), p. 13.

[T]he first lesson we must learn is this, that the work is not initially ours at all, but His. It is not that we work for God, but that He works for us. God gives us our position of rest. He brings His Son's finished work and presents it to us, and then He says to us, 'Please sit' . . . From this point onwards Christian experience proceeds as it began, not on the basis of our own work but always on that of the finished work of Another. Every new spiritual experience begins with the acceptance by faith of what God has done – with a new 'sitting down', if you like.[9]

To be seated with Christ, then, means to recognise our position in Christ, and to realise that God has done everything for us in Christ, resting in the enjoyment and benefits of his work on our behalf. We allow him to take the strain, and just as we would entrust our whole weight to a chair, so we entrust ourselves to him:

To sit down is simply to rest our whole weight – our load, ourselves, our future, everything – upon the Lord. We let Him bear the responsibility and cease to carry it ourselves.[10]

With this understanding of how God intends us to live the Christian life firmly rooted within us, we can truly experience the rest of God. We are free to be at leisure from ourselves. Taking time out to be still and quiet before the Lord will become basic to the way we live and work, a joyful priority rather than a reluctant concession. We will be able to pace ourselves better, and be more able to disentangle ourselves from extraneous demands. We will develop a greater peace within, and be more able to centre

---

[9] Watchmen Nee, *Sit, Walk, Stand* (Victory Press, 1957), p. 14.
[10] *Ibid.*

ourselves on God. And when the opportunity comes to sit and be still, we shall be able to do so in the knowledge that we are sitting down on the inside too!

FOR REFLECTION

1. Does anything prevent you from enjoying outer still-ness? Is there anything you can do to bring more stillness into your life?
2. Why do you think inner stillness is even more elusive? Is it elusive for you? Why might this be?
3. How can you give yourself permission to be still? Does the idea of a sabbath help?
4. What do you think it means for you personally to work from a place of rest?

10

Silence

If we live in a busy world, we also live in a very noisy one. Activity and noise seem to go together, and they surround us. Those of us who are extroverts happily go along with this, finding a buzz from our involvement in the world out there, while others of a more introvert tendency long for more peace and quiet and simply to be able to withdraw for a time. Whatever our natural disposition, each of us needs sufficient space to ourselves so that our spirits can be recreated and renewed. And one thing all the great writers on the subject of the spiritual life stress is that silence is indispensable to a deepening relationship with God. The question is how to be silent and to find silence in a noisy world.

Even church is seldom quiet. A traditional evangelical church service is full of words. We sing words, pray words, read words and preach words – and then have the notices! Seldom is there any space to be still and listen to God. If there is silence it is usually a planned silence, stilted and awkward, like a minute's silence at a football match. Many churches have little awareness of the power of silence, or how to use it creatively within their worship.

Charismatic meetings are very similar. Sometimes it feels

as if the presence of the Spirit can only be measured in decibels, as music groups, complete with amplifiers and sound systems, blast out the latest catchy tunes, and enthusiastic believers sing and clap their hearts out. Open times of worship and prayer encourage participation with loud 'Amens' and 'Hallelujahs'. Occasionally a gentler spirit prevails, but even then silence seems unwelcome, interpreted as a sign of non-involvement on the part of the congregation, or as an indication that nothing is happening and God is not there. Of course the Scriptures encourage us to praise God, and to do so with enthusiasm, but they also tell us that God is just as often present in the still, small voice.

Generally speaking, we are uncomfortable with silence. We do not know what to do with it, and do not appreciate its value. We are embarrassed and unnerved by it. When there is a pause in the conversation, or a gap in the flow of prayer, some of us feel obliged to say or do something. We cannot rest in silence, and always look for ways to cover it up with noise.

This was certainly my own experience. I never knew what to do in times of silence, and found any interval for quiet both long and boring! The idea of a silent retreat was incomprehensible to me. However, since coming to understand the meaning and value of silence, I have begun to appreciate it increasingly and to welcome it into my life. There are times when it is like water to a thirsty soul!

Silence can be regarded as one of the main disciplines of the spiritual life.[1] The apostle James warns us clearly about

---

[1] See Richard Foster, *Celebration of Discipline* (Hodder & Stoughton, 1980) for an excellent introduction to the place and value of the spiritual disciplines, and in particular that of solitude.

the dangers of a careless tongue, and most of us know from first-hand experience what damage can be caused by careless words (James 3:1–12). Being able to control our words is therefore essential, and choosing to be silent is a mark of maturity. As Arsenius said, 'I have often repented of having spoken, but never of having been silent.'[2]

There is a time to speak out about injustice, inequality and so on, but the point we are making here is that our words have a way of running away with themselves and doing great damage. Words once spoken can seldom be taken back. We know that where words are many, transgression is not lacking, and that the person who holds their tongue is considered wise (Proverbs 10:19). By imposing on ourselves the discipline of not speaking, we begin the process of taming the tongue: 'The most frequent argument for silence is simply that words lead to sin. Not speaking, therefore, is the most obvious way to stay away from sin.'[3]

There is a time to speak and a time to be silent, and we need the discernment to know the difference. It is interesting to notice that on occasions Jesus remained silent. When brought before his accusers he refused to defend himself by justifying his actions (Matthew 26:63). Richard Foster recognises that we often use words to manipulate situations and people, and to adjust what others think of us. We are tempted to vindicate ourselves or to retaliate. It requires great spiritual discipline to be silent and to rest our case with God. He rightly points out that 'one of the fruits of silence is the freedom to let our justification rest with God'[4].

---

[2] Quoted in Henri Nouwen, *The Way of the Heart* (DLT, 1981), p. 43.

[3] *Ibid.*, p. 50.

[4] Richard Foster, *Celebration of Discipline* (Hodder & Stoughton, 1980), p. 86.

In developing a mature Christian character, one of our aims is therefore to learn when to speak and when to refrain from speaking (see Proverbs 25:11 and Ecclesiastes 5:2). Only someone who is secure in God knows when it is right to say something and not be silent, and when it is better to remain silent and say nothing.

This ability to be silent and to listen to others is a skill that underpins many other important activities, especially in pastoral care and counselling. It is not just a matter of giving advice and offering our words of wisdom. Often what people need most is simply a listening ear, and to be a good listener we have to learn how to be silent ourselves. Sometimes the best thing we can offer people is not our words, but our silence.

Choosing to be silent is not a negative strategy. It has a positive aim. When we take time to be still and quiet before God, it is a way of opening ourselves up to him and allowing him access to our lives. In stillness we cease our activity; in silence we stop our talking. Both allow God the empty space where he can draw near to us and begin a deeper work in our lives. Both silence and stillness are recreative, and merely sitting for a few moments without saying or doing anything will greatly enrich us. The spiritual part of us will be nourished, and we will be better equipped to deal with the demands and pressures of life. Our souls will be fed and revitalised through the simple discipline of being quiet. Silence prepares us to go deeper with God.

Silence can also be seen as our appropriate response to the presence of God. When God is present the best thing for us to do is to remain silent.

The Lord is in his holy temple; let all the earth be silent before him. (Habakkuk 2:20)

Be silent before the Sovereign Lord. (Zephaniah 1:7)

Be still, and know that I am God. (Psalm 46:10)

Human words become inadequate and inappropriate when God draws near to us. There is a great temptation to say something, but words are not necessary at such a moment. We must beware of talking for the sake of it, like Peter did at the transfiguration, and where it was said of him: 'He did not know what he was saying' (Luke 9:33). To interject human words at such a time is to tarnish the moment.

This was something I learned during a retreat with a group of fellow church leaders. We had begun a time of prayer, and as usual I had started to pray for various situations in the church, trying as best I could to come up with a solution for each problem and then to ask God to act accordingly. In the midst of my prayer I heard God say to me – as clearly as I have heard him say anything – 'Tony, please be quiet.' I knew in that instant that it would be wrong for me to continue praying as I had been doing. I shared briefly with the others what had happened, and we stopped our vocal prayer. A deep silence enveloped us and gripped us for the next 20 minutes. We were transfixed, hardly moving a muscle, unable to say anything. It was the most profound silence I have ever experienced. Words, especially human words, were totally out of place. It wasn't necessary to say or do anything. All that God required of us in that moment was simply to be; to rest before him while he held us in his presence. We knew he had already heard our prayers; that he had everything in hand. We simply basked in his love.

That morning my understanding of silence was totally changed. I saw the difference between a God-given silence and an artificial, man-made silence. Our worship and prayer will bring us so far towards God, but there comes a moment when we have reached his presence (the Holy of Holies as it were) and then the most appropriate thing for us to do is to kneel in silence before him. Once we have experienced such moments, we long for more. We cannot create them, however, or plan them into our services, for there is a givenness about them. What we can do, though, is to remain open to God, to recognise when he is near, and then respond accordingly.

The kind of prayer I have just described is known as contemplative prayer. It is prayer without words. Contemplative prayer immerses us in the silence of God, and at its most basic can be described as 'loving attentiveness to God'[5]. Alexander Ryrie explains it more fully:

> [W]e are content simply to be with God, without inner words, and without requests, demands or expectations. With the silence of the spirit we cease to 'pray' in the usual sense of that word. Being still in the presence of God we acknowledge that our prayer comes not from ourselves but from God. In the prayer of silence it is God who prays within us, and we wait for him.[6]

While we need to make ourselves silent as a preliminary to this form of prayer, at a deeper level it is really a matter of entering into a silence that already exists. It has been said that silence is one way of describing the being of God, and we often speak of the silence of eternity. Certainly we can think of God as the Still Centre of the universe. Contemplative prayer is built around the understanding

---

[5] See Richard Foster, *Prayer* (Hodder & Stoughton, 1992), p. 166, and in particular the whole chapter on contemplative prayer.
[6] Alexander Ryrie, *Silent Waiting* (Canterbury Press, 1999), p. 132.

that since God is silence, we can know him most intimately through silence. Yes, God speaks to us, and he uses words to do so, but words cannot convey all there is to know about him. To know him most fully we need to embrace (or be embraced by) his silence.

Within such silence communion takes place. Communication is based on words, but communion is based on relationship. The closer we are to someone, and the more confident we are with them, the more we can enjoy a companionable silence. This is the intimacy of lovers or the closest of friends. Words are not always needed. Silence is comfortable because we are at ease and the relationship is secure. There is no need to ask anything, no need to explain, no need to impress. We can simply enjoy being together. This is the kind of communion that God seeks with us, and which we can experience through his grace. It is the kind of spiritual intimacy illustrated in the Song of Songs which exists between the Beloved and the one he loves. When we are still and quiet we create an open, empty space where God can draw near and embrace us in his love; where we too can draw near to God and embrace him in our love.

While words are not necessary in communion, it is often in times of silence that God chooses to speak, and it is in such a context that we can most easily hear his voice. One of the reasons for our being silent is that we more readily hear what God has to say:

> Though silence sometimes involves the absence of speech it always involves the act of listening. Simply to refrain from talking, without a heart listening to God, is not silence.[7]

---

[7] Richard Foster, *Celebration of Discipline* (Hodder & Stoughton, 1980), p. 86.

What we 'hear' may not be actual words but rather a holy hunch or an impression. In the stillness we may also hear God's heartbeat, feel his breath, sense his holiness, or know ourselves found, forgiven, restored, re-energised, equipped for service or just simply loved. Even as God whispers such words of love, affirmation or encouragement to us, then maybe we find we are given the words that express more fully our love for him.

When we are still before God, and attuned to his Spirit, we may be given the words we need for others. Words that are born out of silence have greater power than those that flow freely and easily but without much depth. Not only do we hear God for ourselves, we hear what he would have us say to others too. Our words can take on a prophetic edge, simply because we have been still in his presence and listened to him. In this sense, silence teaches us to speak. 'A word with power is a word that comes out of silence.'[8]

At the same time, it must be said that contemplative prayer has value whether or not we hear God speaking to us. It is enough for us simply to be in God's presence whether or not we receive anything from him. Indeed, those schooled in contemplative prayer would suggest that it is sufficient for us simply to be still before God, and that we should not seek any feedback or feeling of getting anywhere, or of hearing the voice of God. This cuts right across the charismatic desire for direct experience of God with specific content and immediate significance, and may therefore be one of the most difficult aspects of contemplative prayer for some of us to grasp.

Henri Nouwen, with his long experience of teaching people how to develop the inner life, strongly encourages

---

[8] Henri Nouwen, *The Way of the Heart* (DLT, 1981), p. 56.

the practice of silence. He says we live in a 'wordy world', where there are too many words spoken and written, and where the greatest danger for ministers is the temptation towards too many words. According to Nouwen, silence protects the spiritual fire within, and we must guard it by not speaking too much and thereby cheapening our words:

> Silence guards the inner heat of religious emotions. The inner heat is the life of the Holy Spirit within us. Thus silence is the discipline by which the inner fire of God is tended and kept alive.[9]

When we are so used to sharing with others what God is doing in our life, this advice may seem surprising, but there is wisdom in it. Sometimes we need to take time to meditate on what God is saying and doing in our lives so that we fully understand it ourselves. And sometimes it is better to hold on to a word from God until the time is right to share it. We can dissipate the power and presence of God in our life by being too quick with our words. Silence enables us to reflect on the events of life and to derive spiritual meaning from them. Like Mary at the birth of Jesus, we need to treasure up some things in our hearts, and ponder them at our leisure (Luke 2:19).

Perhaps now it is easier to see why silence is so indispensable to the growth and development of our spiritual lives. Silence moves us away from the surface of life into the deeper reaches of the heart and spirit. It opens us up to the movement of God by his Spirit. 'Now to tread the spiritual path we must learn to be silent. What is required of us is a journey into profound silence.'[10]

---

[9] Henri Nouwen, *The Way of the Heart* (DLT, 1981), p. 53.
[10] John Main, from an extract in Foster and Griffin, *Spiritual Classic* (HarperCollins, 1999), p. 178.

Silence does not come easily to some of us, and we have to learn first how to befriend our silence. Once we begin to understand and appreciate the power and potential of silence, though, we will yearn for it. Time to be alone with God will become a priority. This will not be a selfish running away from the world or our responsibilities, but an opportunity to be re-energised and renewed in order that we may serve even more effectively. We may end up doing less, but what we do will be more fruitful. It will bring us closer to God and to his heart. Being centred on him will create in us a greater ability to engage with the world, and to make a difference.

As I write this I am reminded of my first experience of a silent retreat. I had arranged to spend time with David and Joyce Huggett at their lovely home in Derbyshire. Although I would meet with one of them on a daily basis, most of the time would be spent alone and in silence. It had been planned for several months, but when the time came I found myself not wanting to go. If I could have found an honourable way out, I would have taken it.

As I packed beforehand, I remember thinking, 'This is not a good idea!' I didn't feel at all in the right frame of mind. There seemed to be so much work to be done, and I felt guilty about leaving it all behind. 'How can I go away and leave it all, just to be quiet?' I asked myself.

Furthermore, it had not been a good time for me spiritually. I hardly felt in the mood for a retreat. My emotions were all over the place, and I could only see me getting even more depressed if I were left alone. My normal way of coping with stress is to be with other people, not on my own. I wondered how I would manage being cut off from my family, with no television or newspapers, and none of my favourite reading material. As I set off, it felt as if I were going into exile! I consoled myself by thinking I could always leave early if I didn't like it.

Joyce greeted me on arrival, and her warm, accepting smile told me I was very welcome. Something inside me said, 'Maybe it won't be so bad after all.' After settling in, and a brief chapel service, I was left to my own devices for the first part of the evening. I sat and relaxed in the sitting room, its windows overlooking the beautiful Derbyshire hills. There was silence all around me, and in the stillness something totally unexpected happened to me. I felt God come to me, and his presence rest upon me. It was completely out of the blue as far as I was concerned, and absolutely unmerited. It was a special gift from God the Father to one of his very needy children. It marked the beginning of three days of wonderful intimacy with God, made all the more special because it was so totally unexpected and so totally undeserved. I could not believe the transformation that took place inside of me. I wrote in my journal, 'If you can't come to the Silence, let the Silence come to you. It has a way of creeping in; of creeping up on you. In a silent place you begin to feel quiet inside. Even if you arrive agitated, let the Silence come to you.'

The retreat was a turning point for me. From that time onwards I discovered the value of silence, and what can happen when we learn to befriend it. It opened a doorway for me into another realm of Christian experience.

FOR REFLECTION

1. Are you comfortable with silence? If not, ask yourself why this might be.
2. Is it appropriate to speak of God as the Still Centre of the universe? What do you think it means?

3. Which of the benefits of silence described here are you familiar with? Which, if any, are new to you? Which would you like to experience more of?
4. How might you befriend your silence?

11

Solitude

Stillness and silence thrive best in a context of solitude. In other words, if I am to be truly still, and able to wait silently before God, I will need at some point to spend time alone. Of course we can seek God in the company of others, and indeed there is a corporate dimension to knowing God, but in order to develop my own inner life fully I will need to withdraw for a while from other people and the normal routine, so that I can meet with God at a deeper, more intimate level.

> The call to solitude is the call to centre our lives deeply and radically in the heart of God alone. It is not a rejection of activity or busyness as such. Solitude will give our lives a firm foundation.[1]

In the history of the church, people have always sought communion with God in quiet and lonely places. They have responded to the call to get away from people in order to spend time with God. In the biblical setting, the desert pro-

---

[1] David Runcorn, *Space for God* (Daybreak, 1990), p. 43.

vided an ideal place to be alone. Jesus often withdrew to the lonely places, and we think of Moses and Elijah, whose ministries involved the desert. John the Baptist was shaped by the wilderness, and the apostle Paul spent three lonely years in the wastelands of Arabia as he came to grips with what God was doing in his life.

The Desert Fathers in the early centuries of the church's existence deliberately went into the desert for solitary prayer and silence. There they sought God and engaged the powers of darkness. Far from being an eccentric bunch (apart from one or two!), they developed deep insights into the ways of God and became famed for their wisdom. Even today their teachings inspire those who look for spiritual wisdom and guidance.[2] Likewise, the continuing existence of monastic orders bears witness to the understanding that aloneness is an integral part of the spiritual life. They particularly value solitude within the context of community. Within their traditions they hold a rich heritage of Christian truth and wisdom often overlooked by evangelicals, but from which we can certainly profit.

Far from being escapist, the purpose of solitude is to better equip us to engage with the world. We are not running away from things, but seeking to gain a better perspective. We are not seeking to avoid responsibility, but to be strengthened for the task. Solitude is not separation. There is a measured detachment, but only for a time, and never a withdrawal of love or involvement. We disengage only in order that we might more effectively re-engage.

---

[2] See Henri Nouwen, *The Way of the Heart* (DLT, 1981). 'The Desert Fathers, who lived in the Egyptian Desert during the fourth and fifth centuries, can offer us a very important perspective on our life as ministers living at the end of the twentieth century' (p. 13).

Some people enjoy their own company, and the idea of solitude holds no fears for them. Others of us are more gregarious and need people around us. Our extrovert lives are full of people, places and projects. We dread loneliness. The prospect of time alone (even with God) does not fill us with excitement. Rather we feel apprehensive.

Without realising it, many of us are uncomfortable with ourselves, which is why we do not enjoy being alone. One of the first things solitude does is to help us face ourselves. Our noise and activity are all part of our cleverly constructed defence systems. Once these are removed, and we are alone before God, we can feel terribly exposed. It is this inner loneliness that God wants to help us with. Rather than look to meeting its aching need through other people, we begin to realise that it can only be met fully in God himself. Solitude is part of the process by which we develop a greater attachment to God and a less possessive hold on other people. As one prayer puts it:

> Show me how to approach my sense of being alone and cut off so that it may not be any longer a condition to be dreaded, but rather seen as a means to closer dependence upon you. Let my soul learn in solitude the lesson of your presence.[3]

Chosen times of solitude, therefore, have a way of refining us. They contain what the Quaker tradition calls 'the sifting silence' – disturbing to experience, but the kind of clearing out of our spiritual systems that Love requires, and which in our higher moments we know we need. Someone called it solitary refinement! We may find that hidden things begin

---

[3] From *When Lonely, A Book of Private Prayer*, quoted in Paul Iles, *Touching the Far Corner* (Bible Society, 1996).

to surface within us too – buried resentments, old wounds, long-forgotten hurts. We may well begin to see our own twisted motives, and in retrospect feel regret at some of our actions and attitudes. Issues we thought were dealt with long ago may surface with renewed energy. It may well feel as if God has taken the lid off our inner world.

Janice had always had a difficult relationship with her father. A solitary man, he was uncommunicative and seldom expressed affection. Janice felt rejected, and a deep resentment built up inside her. Her father was also harsh towards her mother, and Janice often found herself defending her mother from his verbal attacks. After she became a Christian, Janice sought a better relationship with her father. Tearfully, she apologised for her attitude towards him. He made no response, gave no reply and never even acknowledged her presence. She did everything in her power to put things right. She repented, and as best she could forgave him. She received prayer for her own inner hurts. However, she still felt a continuing need to talk about her father, and to blame him for his behaviour. Then, some ten years after he had died, God stepped in.

Janice was spending time alone. Her house overlooked some beautiful Scottish hills, and as she drank in the splendour, she began to pray. As she prayed, she began to cry. She cried and cried, and as she did God began to heal the hurts inside her, and to set her free from the need to constantly criticise her father. God did for her in solitude what she could not do for herself. She was transformed through the silence. Today she can talk freely about her father and acknowledge his weakness without any trace of bitterness or the need to condemn him.

Henri Nouwen regards this as one of the main blessings of solitude. For him it is the furnace of transformation, where God takes away the false scaffolding that surrounds our lives, and strips us of our unhelpful dependency on the things of the world. Solitude is not primarily a place for privacy, or even rest and renewal.

> Rather, it is the place of conversion, the place where the old self dies and the new self is born, the place where the emergence of the new man and the new woman occurs.[4]

Nouwen particularly encourages ministers to free themselves from the 'compulsions' of ministry (the temptation to be relevant, spectacular and powerful) and to face up to their own nothingness. Only then can the struggle with self give way to the transforming encounter with Jesus that leads to fruitful ministry.

The sight of God (and the blessing that accompanies it) is reserved for the pure in heart, and we should not be at all surprised if a deep cleansing work accompanies a determined desire to know God better. Repentance is always met with forgiving grace. If God wounds, he also binds up (see Hosea 6:1–2), and always with the purpose that we may live in his presence.

> When we are willing to wait in solitude and silent prayer before God, the Holy Spirit begins to re-centre our lives, picking through all the distracted fragments and confusion, to the heart of who we are, to the place where God's love waits to welcome us. There we wait in hope and longing for the unfolding of the great secret, kept in God's love – the secret of who we are, in the image of the One who created us.[5]

---

[4] Henri Nouwen, *The Way of the Heart* (DLT, 1981), p. 27.
[5] David Runcorn, *Space for God* (Daybreak, 1990), p. 23.

This recentring of our lives seems to be one of the basic and central aspects of the spiritual life. Our search for God includes the search for ourselves. The two cannot be disentangled. In finding him, we find ourselves; in knowing him, we know ourselves. We know, and are known (Galatians 4:9). There is a deep place within each of us which the Bible calls the 'heart', and it is the heart that longs for God. When Scripture says that 'deep calls to deep' (Psalm 42:7) it is this resonance that it describes; this deep-seated hunger and desire to be united with God, the source of our being. As Richard Foster says:

> Perhaps somewhere in the subterranean chambers of your life you have heard the call to deeper, fuller living. Perhaps you have become weary of frothy experiences and shallow teaching. Every now and then you have caught the glimpses, hints of something more than you have known. Inwardly, you have longed to launch out into the deep.[6]

Solitude allows us to reach out to God in this way. It gives us the opportunity to reflect, and the time and space to meditate on God and his word. It is the cradle of contemplative spirituality. Not only are we able to meet ourselves at a new depth, we can also meet God in a deeper way.

Silence and solitude provide the setting for some of the deeper forms of prayer: the prayer of rest (the Sabbath prayer), the prayer of the heart (the Abba prayer) and contemplative prayer (the prayer of loving attentiveness). Each is described in full by Richard Foster in his book called

---

[6] Richard Foster, *Celebration of Discipline* (Hodder & Stoughton, 1980), p. 2.

simply *Prayer*.[7] Each describes a way of praying by which we draw near to God without the use of words. We rest ourselves in God, delight in his fatherly care and gaze upon his beauty.

> In solitude we voluntarily abstain from our normal patterns of activity and inter-action with people for a time in order to discover that our strength and well-being come from God alone . . . In experiences of solitude we gently press into the Holy of Holies, where we are sifted in the stillness. Painfully, we let go of the vain images of ourselves in charge of everything and everybody. Slowly we loosen our grip on all those projects that to us seem so significant. Gently we become more focussed and simplified. Joyfully, we receive the nourishment of heavenly manna.[8]

For some there may well be experiences of deep intimacy, even of spiritual ecstasy. Union with God is the goal of contemplative prayer. Not all have such experiences, however, and they should not become an end in themselves. Sometimes, because of the nature of God's working within us, we may find ourselves void of feelings, experiencing what was described by St John of the Cross as 'the dark night of the soul'.[9] At such moments God's presence has to be known in his absence. Paradoxically, presence and absence go together. Much as we would like to experience

---

[7] Richard Foster, *Prayer* (Hodder & Stoughton, 1992). See Part II, 'Moving Upward: seeking the intimacy we need', chs 9, 12, 14.

[8] *Ibid.*, p. 105.

[9] See *The Cloud of Unknowing* (Hodder & Stoughton, 1996 translation). This anonymous work, over 500 years old, remains one of the best guides to the interior life and the higher forms of contemplative prayer.

good feelings all the time, these are the gift of God and cannot be brought about by our own efforts. They cannot be produced, only waited for. God remains a mystery, and never comes under our control.

For Andrew this was in fact the way he discovered the value of contemplative prayer. An active and committed member of a house church, Andrew experienced for the first time a long period of spiritual darkness, which he found difficult to understand. It was his inability to pray using words during this time, and the sense of the absence of God, which led him to pray without words. With the help of a spiritual director he began to realise that this 'dark night of the soul' was in fact quite normal, and not at all a sign that he had backslidden. This came as a great relief to him, for within his evangelical background he had no framework to understand such an experience.

Evangelicals and charismatics often feel a great pressure to be experiencing God and hearing his voice all the time. There is little understanding of what to do when this doesn't happen. Many feel guilty at such times, thinking they are failing in their walk with God, when in fact God is entrusting them with the opportunity to deepen their faith and to trust him even when there are no tangible signs of his presence.

Times of regular solitude are essential to effective ministry. Nouwen goes so far as to say that real ministry flows out of solitude, for ministry can and must be the result of direct and intimate encounter with Jesus. In solitude, ministry and spirituality meet each other. As we meet with God and allow him to transform us, compassion is born into our hearts. We can feel the pain of others because we have felt our own pain. We can understand their brokenness because we have encountered our own. Compassion then is the fruit of our solitude and becomes the basis of our ministry to others. Those who have been forgiven much, love much.

> What becomes visible here is that solitude moulds self-righteous people into gentle, caring, forgiving persons who are so deeply convinced of their own great sinfulness and so fully aware of God's even greater mercy that their life itself becomes ministry.[10]

In solitude we do not move away from people. Instead our hearts draw closer to them. We learn to identify ourselves with them, and with the whole world.

How do we find this solitude? Sometimes solitude is not so much chosen as given. The circumstances of life may cause us to be isolated, cut off and alone. We may not choose such events, nor welcome them, but they provide a wonderful opportunity for us to learn solitude.

Audrey had been working for the British Embassy in Cambodia. It was a period of intense activity for her, both in her working life and at home. When the opportunity came up for a holiday in the UK, the family could hardly wait. However, within ten days of arriving home Audrey was struck down with a violent attack of dengue fever.

One day, as she was lying in bed, too weak to do anything else, God spoke to her: 'Is this what I have to do to get you to be still and listen to me?' Audrey was shocked. She had thought that by being the good 'all-round mum', she was doing what God wanted. But no, God was right. Somewhere in her busyness, and in looking out for and organising everyone else, she had lost the peaceful place in the middle of her heart which belonged to God.

Slowly, as she started to recover, she began to read *Open*

---

[10] Henri Nouwen, *The Way of the Heart* (DLT, 1981), p. 37.

to God by Joyce Huggett.[11] As she read, a small revolution took place within her. She began to realise that it was permissible to stop and listen to God – in fact it was essential. She began to learn a new kind of prayer, contemplative prayer, whereby she was content to wait before God in silence. Gradually she regained her perspective and excitement at knowing the living God. It became a defining moment in her relationship with God. When she returned to Cambodia some weeks later she was full of joy and enthusiasm because of all that God had done for her.

At other times solitude is a choice, and we must make our own space. It may come in the little intervals of our day that provide us with aloneness; it may be through the regular daily discipline of time spent with God; it may be by means of a planned withdrawal for a retreat or quiet day. However it happens, it is vital that we fashion our own piece of desert and make it a meeting place with God – an opportunity to get away with Jesus.

For reflection

1. How do you feel about spending time alone? If you feel negative about it, ask yourself why this might be.
2. Have you ever experienced a 'dark night of the soul'? What did you learn from it?
3. Is there an enforced solitude in your life at this moment? If so, how can you use it to your spiritual advantage?
4. How can you create solitude in your own life?

---

[11] Joyce Huggett, *Open to God* (Hodder & Stoughton, 1989).

Keep Company with Me

Having responded to the invitation of Jesus to be with him, we now consider how to develop our friendship with him. What will take us deeper in our relationship with him? What will help us to know him more fully? Here we look at three of the disciplines of grace; practical means by which the life of Christ can be imparted to us. They are reflection, meditation and contemplation. We are called to think carefully about our lives and how we live; to consider well what God is saying to us in Scripture and creation; and to dwell in his presence, gazing upon him and drinking in his beauty. Once again there is a measure of overlap between the three, but sufficient distinctiveness for us to consider them individually.

To the Silent Heart

Some of the deepest prayers ever prayed are prayers of
   silence.
Being in My Presence, saying nothing and wanting nothing,
   is a prayer.
Being together, letting our Presences merge and our wills
   blend, is a prayer.
Two hearts, beating as ONE, is a prayer.

Stay with Me in the silence
while I look at you and you look at Me.

Angela Ashwin

12

Reflection

We were coming to the end of a time of prayer in our house group, and had reached the point where we felt comfortable to sit in silence for a moment or two. The house was unusually quiet. As we sat in the stillness, the only sound we could hear was the clock above the fireplace. Tick, tock, tick, tock. So rhythmic, so faithful in its routine. It occurred to me that most days no one in that house would ever actually hear the clock, although it was always ticking away reliably. Most days its sound would be obscured by the everyday noise of normal family living. But in this moment, because we were stilled, we were able to hear its sound.

God is always speaking to us. Faithfully, day by day, his word goes forth. Often, because of our busyness and hustle and bustle, we do not hear what he is saying to us. Only when we still ourselves can we hear his quiet, gentle, insistent whisper. Reflection is one of the means by which we teach ourselves to hear the word that is all around us.

The ability to reflect is the ability to think backwards. In the mental process of reflection, we are able to recall events and consider their significance; to recognise what is happening in our lives. As we take time to think over things, we can evaluate and analyse them, enjoying again the positive aspects, learning from our mistakes and drawing from them lessons for the future so their impact is not lost or wasted. It is easy to see why reflection is an integral part of developing the inner life.

When Jesus commanded his disciples to remember him through the breaking of bread, he was encouraging them to make the discipline of reflection part of their normal life. He was suggesting that they regularly pause in their routine in order to think back over the events of his death, so that they would not lose the significance of what he had done for them.

Later on, the apostle Paul suggested another reflective activity in preparation for this – that of examining oneself before partaking. Taking time to think over one's life and behaviour is a safeguard against eating and drinking unworthily (1 Corinthians 11:28). It is a discipline that needs to be cultivated in a world where we dash from one activity to another with little or no thought for the significance of what we are doing. Self-examination need not be a negative exercise. It is as much about recognising what we have done right as about what we may have done wrong; and in the context of God's unconditional and unchanging love for us, we dare to face up to our mistakes and shortcomings since we know there is forgiveness and acceptance. Only thus can we be transformed and grow in Christian character.

Throughout the Old Testament the Jews were also encouraged to 'remember' what God had done for them, especially in bringing them out of slavery in Egypt. By stopping and reflecting on where they had come from, and on the mighty acts of God, they would be protected from the ever present danger of wandering away from the Lord:

> Remember how the Lord your God led you all the way in the
> desert these forty years, to humble you and to test you in order
> to know what was in your heart, whether or not you would
> keep his command. (See Deuteronomy 8:1–20, especially v.2)

By consciously looking back and considering their history, their love would be rekindled, their faith would be strengthened and their understanding of God's ways would be increased.

The prophets also called Israel to be a reflective people in order to avoid the spiritual apathy that so often dogged their progress. Haggai, for instance, rallied the people of his day who had largely ignored the interests of God in favour of their own concerns, with the call: 'Give careful thought to your ways' (Haggai 1:5,7). Only by reflecting on their lives and honestly examining their ways would they be able to recognise how far they had slipped away from God. Only by taking a close look at what was happening in their lives would they be able to recognise that the blessing of God was no longer with them. In the hurly-burly of activity they could easily have missed the message that was there for them in the circumstances of their lives.

Likewise, after they had rebuilt the foundation of the Temple, the prophet calls on them not to lose the significance of the event: 'From this day on . . . give careful thought to the day when the foundation of the Lord's temple was laid. Give careful thought . . .' (Haggai 2:18). Experience was to be their teacher, but they would only learn the lessons if they reflected on what had happened. By giving careful consideration to all that had taken place, they would be able to learn from their mistakes and ultimately profit from them. Often we fail to learn the lessons God has for us simply because we do not take time to reflect.

Spiritual truth is absorbed largely through the process of reflection. Not only do we need to hear the truth, but we must take time to think it over and consider its implications for our lives. So the apostle Paul exhorts Timothy: 'Reflect on what I am saying, for the Lord will give you insight into all this' (2 Timothy 2:7). Here we see the biblical way to spiritual understanding. As we humbly reflect in our minds, the Holy Spirit grants revelation in our hearts. The two processes go together and are inseparable. We do not arrive at spiritual understanding through our own ability. We are dependent upon revelation from God, and he rarely grants such revelation in a vacuum. He gives it to those who take time to sit and think about his word. It is the reflective person, therefore, who will be best placed to grow in spiritual understanding. As John Stott comments:

> For the understanding of Scripture a balanced combination of thought and prayer is essential. We must do the considering, and the Lord will do the giving of understanding.[1]

One contemporary author who has brought to our attention again the importance of reflection is the American writer, Ken Gire. Through his books *The Reflective Life* and *Windows of the Soul* he urges us to adopt a more reflective approach to living, in order that we may hear more clearly the voice of God. It is through reflection that we can recognise God's voice in the circumstances of life. His word is all around us – in our life events, in Scripture, in books, in the theatre or cinema, in countless ordinary places – if we would but recognise it:

---

[1] John Stott, *Guard the Gospel* (IVP, 1973), p. 60.

The reflective life is a life that is attentive, receptive, and responsive to what God is doing in us and around us. It's a life that asks God to reach into our heart, allowing Him to touch us there, regardless of the pleasure it excites or the pain it inflicts.[2]

The reflective life makes us aware of the sacred that surrounds us but which often we do not see. In order to live more reflectively, we need to slow down. To truly benefit from what God is saying to us or doing in our lives, we need to stop and pause. Only then will we recognise and respond to those God-given moments that come to each of us in the course of our daily lives.

Living reflectively provides opportunities during our day for a closer look at things, at people, at ourselves, and at God. The faster the pace of life, though, the more we will miss those opportunities.[3]

By slowing down we are able to see what is sacred and to recognise the presence and activity of God in the ordinariness of our own lives.

On one retreat I attended we were asked to do an 'awareness walk'. We were encouraged to walk in the grounds where we were staying and to use our senses to encounter God. The retreat leader suggested we look carefully and in detail at what was around us, noticing things we might otherwise miss. We were to listen to the sounds we may not normally hear, and 'feel' what was there in the garden.

It was a crisp autumn morning. I was surprised how

---

[2] Ken Gire, *The Reflective Life* (Kingsway, 1998), p. 11.
[3] *Ibid.*, p. 25.

readily God spoke to me, and how easy it became to pray. I came across a shrub with some colourful berries, the kind that birds love to eat in winter. It reminded me how God provides for them (and us), and how the birds scatter the tiny seeds, causing the plant to grow elsewhere. I thought of Christians being scattered by circumstances and taking the gospel with them, and prayed for the spread of the church throughout the world.

Further on I picked up an apple, lying neglected on the ground along with dozens of others that had never been harvested. It made me think of those who had never had the chance to hear the gospel. I prayed that the Lord of the harvest would send labourers into the harvest field, that the fruit would not be lost.

At the bottom of the garden a holly bush was covered in bright red berries, reminding me of Christmas. I thought of my sister, who had sung 'The holly and the ivy' in church as a girl, and prayed for her. I thought too of the Saviour who had shed his blood for each of us, so there might be a gospel to preach.

With very little effort on my part I had enjoyed a time of rich communion with God, simply because I had been encouraged to slow down, notice what was around me and listen for the voice of God. Nature is full of parables, if only we become aware of what is there.

Gire speaks of what he calls three 'habits of the heart', which help us to nurture a reflective life and heighten our awareness of the sacred:

1. Reading the moment – using our eyes to see what is on the surface, actually noticing what is going on around us.
2. Reflecting on the moment – engaging our mind to look beneath the surface, and to consider its significance.

3. Responding to the moment – allowing what we have seen or felt to have a place in our heart, and allowing it to grow there, upward to God and outward towards other people.

Using these three simple steps we can benefit from any God-given moment that occurs in our life, whether it be a chance conversation with another person, something that catches our attention in a book, or even a scene in a film that speaks to us. God is continually planting the seeds of his word into our life, in countless different ways every day. By recognising such moments, reflecting on them and then responding to them, we can capture those heavenly seeds. That which is of eternal significance can then be planted within us.

Journalling

One of the most helpful and practical ways of learning to reflect is to use a journal. A journal is a tool that enables us to open up a dialogue with God about our life. By writing down and recording the things that happen to us, along with our feelings and responses, we are able to reflect honestly about ourselves, and to begin to trace God's hand at work in our lives.

> [Journalling] helps us see what we look at. When we journal, it's like taking a Polaroid of some moment during the day that has caught our attention. Only we do it with words instead of with film. But like that film, what we have looked at often develops right before our very eyes as we're writing, revealing things we hadn't seen before.[4]

---

[4] Ken Gire, *The Reflective Life* (Kingsway, 1998), pp. 92–3.

Christians down the centuries have benefited from journalling, and it is regarded as one of the classic spiritual disciplines. A journal is more than a diary, for its purpose is to record not merely events, but those which are significant. It is a personal record of what is happening inside us, and therefore focuses on our thoughts and feelings. Its purpose is to help us understand ourselves, and to recognise the activity and voice of God in our lives.

> Journalling helps us pay attention to God. It is a way of hearing and responding to God.[5]

> For those who seek to follow Jesus, journals are an ideal way to track their journey and to interact with Jesus along the way. Journals help them to know themselves and God, and to see God at work in the intricacies of their lives.[6]

Journals can be used for many purposes, but have particular relevance for spiritual growth. We can use them to record our thoughts and insights during Bible study, or to make notes of things that puzzle or interest us. We can use them as a prayer diary, recording our requests, noting the outcomes. We can be very honest, confessing our sins, identifying the issues we are struggling with, trying to understand them better as we write. We can think as we write, meditating on our lives and actions, looking back over things that have happened and evaluating them. A journal can be what we want it to be, what we need it to be at any given time. It is a wonderful tool to help us get in touch with our real selves and with our innermost thoughts. It is

---

[5] Richard Peace, *Spiritual Journalling* (NavPress, 1998), p. 7.
[6] *Ibid.*, p. 10.

a safe place, where we can learn to be real and authentic. A journal, well used, will become a trusted friend.

Why is it so helpful to journal in this way? Because the very act of writing down what we are thinking (if we are willing to be honest) is liberating in itself. As we write, our thoughts are clarified, perspective is gained and often insight develops. Things we were afraid of become less threatening when written down. Issues that were confused become clearer. Instead of possibly deceiving ourselves, we are enabled to get in touch with our real selves and to face up to things as they really are:

> In the privacy of personal reflection, insights are received, confessions are offered, progress is noted. Journal writing fosters a careful attention to the soul's condition, and we are better for the tending.[7]

Journals are a powerful tool for exploring the inner world of emotions and feelings. Writing allows us to get in touch with feelings that might otherwise be unhealthily repressed or buried away. Journalling enables us to explore these emotions, and to express them in an appropriate and safe way. Dreams, which are often a clue as to what is going on in our inner lives, can also be recorded and reflected upon.[8]

Through reflective writing we enter into a dialogue with God. Our writing is a conversation with him, and not surprisingly he often has something to say! In the very act of expressing ourselves openly and honestly, God so often

---

[7] Jana Rea, *A Spiritual Formation Journal* (Harper, 1992).
[8] Richard Peace has some helpful comments on how we can learn from our dreams in *Spiritual Journalling* (NavPress, 1998), pp. 64–7.

speaks a word of guidance or reassurance or understanding or acceptance. Communication is at the heart of our relationship with God, and journalling is an aid to both talking and listening to God. When placed within the wider context of being alone with God, journalling becomes a way not only to understand ourselves better, but to love ourselves better as well. Whatever we discover about ourselves, we do so in the knowledge that God loves us unconditionally. We need not be afraid to express ourselves freely when we have the safety net of God's grace beneath us.

Over a period of time journals become a record of our spiritual journey, showing where we have come from, where we are and pointing us to where we may be going. They become a rich source of inspiration to us as we chart the way God has led us, answered our prayers and made provision for us. They become our personal book of psalms.

Richard Peace suggests we can use journalling for other specific purposes, especially in understanding our life history and coming to terms with the past, as well as in thinking about the future and discerning God's will:

> Journalling helps us understand our unfolding story. Knowing our story helps us see what God has been doing in the past, is doing now, and is calling us to do in the future.[9]

One of my friends, Greg, has benefited enormously from journalling. Not by nature a reflective person, he was introduced to the idea by his mentor. He tried it and was amazed how helpful he found it, in particular in working through some of his more negative emotions. Now journalling has

---

[9] Richard Peace, *Spiritual Journalling* (NavPress, 1998), p. 7.

become part of his daily routine. First thing in the morning, while the house is still quiet and the children are asleep, Greg is at work on his journal. Not only does he reflect on how he is feeling, but he notes the things God is saying to him, and keeps a records of things he has read which have helped him. Every now and then he looks back over the things he has written to see if there are any trends or patterns, and to be reminded of important things that have happened.

Socrates said that the unreflective life is not worth living. Certainly lives that are busy and always on the move have a tendency to be shallow and scattered. Those who wish for something more substantial, for something deeper and more focused, must give themselves the time and space to reflect.

For reflection

1. At the end of today, stop and think over everything that has happened. What stands out for you? What was good and what was bad? How can you see God at work in the course of your day?

2. Try an awareness walk. Take about 20 minutes to explore a chosen place. Use all your senses to discover what God the Creator has put there. What do you see? Hear? Smell? What can you touch? Allow God to speak to you through parables of nature.

3. Keep a journal. Simply write down the thoughts and feelings that you have, but write as if you are in God's presence. Maybe write it as a letter to God. Persevere for a few days and see if it helps you to become more reflective. If you find it helpful, continue with this exercise.

13

Bible Meditation (Lectio Divina)

Anyone can meditate. When Isaac went out into the field in the early evening to meditate (Genesis 24:63), he was doing what many of us do instinctively: he was taking a moment to be still and to think his own thoughts. He deliberately chose a quiet part of the day when he could be relaxed, and he found a familiar and lonely place where he would be undisturbed. There, in the tranquillity of the evening, he was free simply to be alone and gather his thoughts. All of us need such re-creating moments in our lives where we can gather ourselves together and bring our scattered thoughts to order. This is the heart of meditation.

While reflection is about thinking backwards, meditation is about thinking deeply. When we meditate, we take time to think through issues, to look at them first this way and then that way. We consider things from different points of view, look at them from different angles. We chew things over in our minds, like a cow chews the cud – going over and over it until our thoughts become clear and settled.

Worry is a form of meditation. When we worry about something we continually dwell on that which is negative and unhelpful. We allow our imagination to run wild, thinking of all the bad things that might happen. Anxious thoughts swirl round and round in our minds. When this happens we are meditating, but unhealthily so. What this shows is that we can all meditate. It is not a matter of intelligence or spiritual prowess. We meditate instinctively. What is important, though, is that we meditate on the right things. We can choose what we meditate upon, and it is possible, with discipline and practice, to turn our minds and attention to more uplifting thoughts.

This is what Mary did at the birth of Jesus. So many wonderful things happened to her in such a short space of time that she couldn't take it all in at once. Rather she stored these things up in her heart, and over a period of time dwelt on them, thinking through the significance of what had taken place in the quietness of her own heart: 'But Mary treasured up all these things and pondered them in her heart' (Luke 2:19). In this way Mary's faith was built up, and she was strengthened within herself. Meditation is one of the main ways by which we can go deeper in spiritual matters. It takes us from the merely surface and superficial into a consideration of more substantial matters. This is why it is regarded as a central part of Christian devotion and a key aspect of contemplative spirituality.

One of the Old Testament words for meditation (*hagah* in the Hebrew) suggests a muttering or speaking quietly to oneself. It seems that meditating in ancient Israel involved repeating or murmuring key texts in a low voice – a kind of reciting of God's word to oneself. This form of meditation was popular with the Desert Fathers, who made the words of the Bible their own by memorising them and repeating them over and over again with deep concentration. In this way the term 'meditation' has come to refer to the use of short repeated prayers said quietly over and over again. This kind of prayer is called a 'rhythm prayer', and is commonly used as a basis for silent or contemplative prayer. The Jesus Prayer ('Lord Jesus Christ, Son of God, have mercy on me, a sinner') is one of the most widely used. Typically such prayers call on God to be present and to have mercy or to grant help. They are repeated constantly, along with the rhythm of one's breathing. As well as helping to reduce distractions, this method of prayer becomes a way for moving the attention from the head to the heart:

> Through this kind of prayer one is taken out of one's thoughts and led into the deepest and most central part of oneself, the heart, the secret, inmost place which no one else can enter, the place where one is most truly oneself.[1]

Such 'prayers of the heart' lead us deeper into God. For many people they become the means of praying continually, and open up a stream of prayer for those who practise this form of meditation diligently.

The other word for meditation in the Old Testament is *suach*, and this describes silent, inward thinking, pondering or reflecting. This kind of meditation usually has an object, and most commonly it is focused upon the word of God. Christian meditation is distinctive in that it is centred on the revelation of God through the Bible.

Meditating on Scripture is different from Bible study, however. In Bible study we seek to analyse the passage and understand it intellectually. When we meditate on Scripture we take just a small portion and seek to internalise it,

---

[1] Alexander Ryrie, Silent Waiting (Canterbury Press, 1999), p. 129. See also his fuller discussion on meditation, pp. 13–7 and pp. 125–30.

making the meaning personal and looking for the way in which it will impact our lives. We are seeking to allow the word of God to sink down from our heads to our hearts, and to transform and change us. We are looking to hear what God has to say to us today as individuals, rather than what he has to say in general to all people at all times.

Thus, with the help of the Holy Spirit, we might take a verse or phrase of Scripture and mull it over in our minds. We look at it this way and then that way, asking the Spirit to give us understanding and revelation. All the time we are seeking to apply the truths we discover to our own life, honestly responding in obedience to what we find there. We are not looking for something to share with others, but rather for what God has to say to us personally.

> We meditate to give God's words the opportunity to penetrate, not just our minds, but our emotions – the places where we hurt – and our will – the place where we make our choices and decisions. We meditate to encounter the Living Word, Jesus himself. We meditate so that every part of our being, our thoughts and our affections and our ambitions, are turned to face and honour and glorify him.[2]

It can easily be seen from this that Christian meditation is very different from other forms of meditation, especially those associated with Eastern religions or Transcendental Meditation. Rather than emptying the mind, Christian meditation is about filling the mind with the word of God; and rather than it being about detachment from everything around us, it is more about attachment – seeking to be joined more closely to Christ and his word. Peter Toon, in

---

[2] Joyce Huggett, Learning the Language of Prayer (BRF, 1994), p. 38.

his book *Meditating as a Christian*, makes this distinction very clear, and even suggests that 'formative reading' may be a better term to use, since the purpose of Christian meditation is to be 'formed' or shaped by the text of Scripture.

> I do not hold the Bible in my hand in order to analyse, dissect or to gather information from it. Rather I hold it in order to let my Master penetrate the depths of my being with his Word and thus facilitate inner moral and spiritual transformation. I am there in utter dependence upon our God – who is the Father to whom I pray, the Son through whom I pray, and the Holy Spirit in whom I pray.[3]

The aim of meditation is of course to meet with Jesus, the Beloved One. We read the Scriptures as a love letter, and approach them carefully and tenderly, savouring each word so that we can find him. We read devotionally, in an attitude of love.

> We perhaps need constantly to remind ourselves that the end and aim of formative reading is to seek Christ in the inspired and sacred text in order to discover the love of God, to savour that love and to be united in faith and love with the Bridegroom of our souls. My soul may be compared to the honey bee who gathers from the sweet, spiritual flowers of God's revelation the divine pollen in order to taste the heavenly sweetness of the salvation which is in Jesus.[4]

Many devotional writers point out the importance of using the imagination when meditating upon the Scriptures. This was particularly the recommendation of

---

[3] Peter Toon, Meditating as a Christian (HarperCollins, 1991), p. 59.
[4] *Ibid.*, p. 62.

Ignatius of Loyola in his Spiritual Exercises. He encouraged
his followers to visualise the Gospels. Richard Foster also
encourages this approach, feeling that 'the inner world of
meditation is most easily entered through the door of the
imagination'[5]. Few people, he suggests, can approach meditation in a purely abstract way. Thus when we meditate on
the Scriptures we should seek to take our place within the
story, and to use our senses to imagine what it was like. By
feeling the story, we can enter into the text and the text can
enter into us.

> Take a single event like the resurrection, or a parable, or a few
> verses, or even a single word and allow it to take root in you.
> Seek to live the experience, remembering the encouragement of
> Ignatius of Loyola to apply our senses to the task . . . Smell the
> sea. Hear the lap of the water along the shore. See the crowd.
> Feel the sun on your head and the hunger in your stomach.
> Taste the salt in the air. Touch the hem of his garment.[6]

This is an approach with which theologian Alister
McGrath is in full agreement. In his book *The Journey*, he
describes his own discovery of the practice of biblical meditation. He says that Western Christianity, influenced by the
Enlightenment and its emphasis on reason, has neglected
the imagination and the emotions. As he began to meditate
on Scripture, he found that as well as *understanding* biblical truth, he was able to *appreciate* it. He began to explore
the theme of projecting oneself into Scripture and allowing
oneself to be caught up in the story.

[5] Richard Foster, *Celebration of Discipline* (Hodder & Stoughton,
1980), p. 22.
[6] *Ibid.*, p. 26.

I had to think of myself as being there, witnessing what was said and done. I began to read the gospel narratives with new excitement . . . Meditating in this way on the gospel text led naturally to an enhanced appreciation of all that Jesus is, and all that He has done for me. It led most naturally into prayer. *Reading the Bible leads to meditating on the Bible, which leads to praying from the Bible.*[7]

While the Scriptures are the main source of material for meditation, they themselves encourage us to broaden our outlook and find God everywhere around us. This is especially so in creation, for God has inscribed many of his most important lessons in the world of nature. Jesus often found spiritual meaning and insight from the everyday things around him, and drew the attention of his disciples to things that were right before their very eyes. 'Look at the birds,' he said. 'Consider the lilies. Think about the grass of the field.'

These were to be the icons [pictures] through which the disciples would penetrate the mystery of God's providence and protection, and discover hidden wisdom and truth about God's relationship with his creation.

The disciples are invited to consider, to notice, to learn from the lilies, not by a peremptory glance but by a long, feasting look. 'Consider' has about it the feeling of restful reflection, leisurely appreciation, a freedom of heart to gaze and wonder, and, in doing so, to discover truth.[8]

---

[7] Alister McGrath, *The Journey* (Hodder & Stoughton, 1999), pp. 16–17. Used by permission of Hodder & Stoughton Ltd.

[8] Margaret Magdalen, *Jesus Man of Prayer* (Eagle, 1987), pp. 24, 23.

Modern life, with all its rushing, leaves little time for this kind of meditation. There is so little opportunity to stop and stare, for 'walking and gawking' (to use one of Joyce Huggett's favourite expressions). We are poorer as a result. Spiritual wisdom often remains hidden from view, yet is all around us. 'Go to the ant you sluggard; consider its ways and be wise' (Proverbs 6:6). Who would have thought that a simple creature like the ant could teach modern, sophisticated man anything? Yet a careful observation of its ways, reveals one of the most profound lessons of life: that nothing is achieved without a willingness to work at it, and that diligence is a quality to be sought after, both in spiritual matters and life in general. And it is not only the ant that can teach us wisdom. Every creature, every bird, every plant, every tree or flower has its own insights to impart to those who have eyes to see.

I was watching some squirrels scampering through the branches of the trees one day. I marvelled at their agility and their ability to know which branches would bear their weight – and these were well-built squirrels that obviously had a large store of nuts somewhere! As they darted here and there, they were so skilful in making their way through the branches and the multiplicity of options available to them. Whether they went up, down, left or right didn't seem to matter to them, as long as they were heading generally in the right direction.

It spoke to me about guidance. Sometimes we feel paralysed by the many choices before us, and are fearful of choosing the wrong option and making a mistake. But we can trust God to lead us in the direction he wants us to take. If we prayerfully commit our way to God beforehand, and desire to do his will, he is able to bring us to the place he wants us to be. If we take a wrong turning, he can always lead us by another way. Ultimately he will guide us into the right path.

Neither should we forget the overall impact that creation can have upon us. As we stand before the majesty of mountains and oceans, deserts and forests, we begin to feel our own smallness. We begin to bring our lives into perspective; to feel a true estimate of our own humanity and finiteness. Such moments encourage in us a sense of humility; of knowing our place within the universe.

> When I consider your heavens,
> the work of your fingers,
> the moon and the stars,
> which you have set in place,
> what is man that you are mindful of him,
> the son of man that you care for him? (Psalm 8:3)

We need to recapture this sense of wonder if it is missing from our lives. We can become so preoccupied with ourselves and our concerns that we lose our sense of proportion. Getting out into the broad open spaces, alone with God in his creation, can have a profoundly restorative effect on us, especially if we allow ourselves to pause and think and reflect.

We can meditate on anything that points us towards God. We can even meditate on the injustice and pain in the world, and ponder the great mysteries of human existence. We can meditate on the events of our time and seek to understand their significance, looking to God for insight and understanding. Some of the great devotional writings of church history provide a tremendous source of spiritual nourishment. We can also follow the exhortation of the apostle Paul and choose those things that are uplifting as we find them in art, music and literature:

Finally, brothers, whatever is true, whatever is noble, whatever is right, whatever is pure, whatever is lovely, whatever is admirable – if anything is excellent or praiseworthy – think about such things. (Philippians 4:8)

Henri Nouwen has written a moving account of how God spoke to him through Rembrandt's painting, 'Return of the Prodigal Son'. He first saw it as a poster in someone's office, and sensed that God was speaking to him through the painting. As he meditated further on it, and visited the museum in Russia where the original is on display, it opened up for him a whole new understanding of what it means to be the beloved of God. It was a transforming experience for him, and since then, through his writings, for many others as well.[9]

The fruits of meditation can be seen in a renewed mind and a changed life. If we allow the word of God to be continually in our minds, it will shape the way we think, and guide the way we behave. If we allow it to sink into our hearts it will become part and parcel of who we are, so that obedience to God will become the most natural thing of all. As a man thinks in his heart, so he is (Proverbs 23:7).

Not surprisingly, meditation easily moves into prayer and opens up a conversation with God. Our meditation takes place in his presence, and soon becomes a meditation of him and with him. We should not take the experience for granted, however. Sometimes we will move easily into the presence of God through our meditation; at other times it may not come so easily. We must remember that it is a divine work, for which we are dependent upon God:

---

[9] Henri Nouwen, *The Return of the Prodigal Son* (DLT, 1994).

Anyone who imagines he can simply begin meditating without praying for the desire and the grace to do so will soon give up. But the desire to meditate, and the grace to begin meditating, should be taken as an implicit promise of further graces.[10]

Meditation will provide rich rewards in our lives. It will draw us closer to God, and bring God closer to us. It is well worth the effort.

Lectio divina

Closely linked to the practice of meditation is an ancient method of Bible reading known as *lectio divina* (pronounced lex-ee-oh di-vee-nuh). It has been followed in the church for nearly fifteen hundred years, being first promoted and encouraged by St Benedict among those who followed his Rule. It is a method that is currently returning to popularity today.

Essentially *lectio divina* is a devotional way of reading the Scriptures where the aim is unashamedly to generate spiritual nourishment rather than academic or intellectual information. The name means literally 'divine reading'. 'Divine' because the subject matter is God's word, and 'reading' since the method involves reading a short passage or verse of Scripture several times. It combines both approaches to meditation that we looked at earlier: the muttering to oneself and the silent inward pondering. The purpose is to hear the voice of God through what is read:

[10] Thomas Merton, 'Spiritual Direction and Meditation', quoted by Richard Foster, *Prayer* (Hodder & Stoughton, 1992), p. 162.

. . . lectio is undertaken in the conviction that God's word is meant to be a 'good' word – that is, something carrying God's own life in a way that is beneficial to the one who receives it faithfully. Lectio turns to the Scripture in order that we may be nourished, comforted, refreshed by it. Lectio is an encounter with the living God. It is prayer.[11]

This is a kind of reading in which the mind descends into the heart, and both are drawn into the love and goodness of God.[12]

The method behind *lectio divina* is quite simple, but very profound. Rather than trying to make sense of the word of God we simply rest and allow it to speak to us. The word we receive then becomes a 'given' word, purely for our own benefit and for the nourishment of our own souls. It touches our heart rather than our head.

Richard Peace, in his book *Contemplative Bible Reading*, describes a four-part movement in *lectio divina*, which I quote in full.

1. Reading/Listening: Read aloud a short passage of scripture. As you read, listen for the word or phrase that speaks to you. What is the Spirit drawing your attention to?
2. Meditating: Repeat aloud the word or phrase to which you are drawn. Make connections between it and your life. What is God saying to you by means of this word or phrase?
3. Praying: Now take these thoughts and offer them back to God in prayer, giving thanks, asking for guidance, asking for forgiveness, and resting in God's love. What is God leading you to pray?

---

[11] Norvene Vest, *Knowing by Heart* (DLT, 1995), p. 3.
[12] Richard Foster, *Prayer* (Hodder & Stoughton, 1992), p. 157.

4. Contemplating: Move from the activity of prayer to the stillness of contemplation. Simply rest in God's presence. Stay open to God. Listen to God. Remain in peace and silence before God. How is God revealing himself to you?[13]

Peace is quick to point out that *lectio divina* is not a substitute for serious Bible study, or for understanding the text in an academic way. Rather it builds upon the analytical approach, and to some extent assumes a reasonable knowledge of the Scripture being thought about. It has a different objective in mind, however: to help us hear God's word through the text, and grow in holiness of life as a result. Certainly it provides a welcome alternative for those who study the Bible professionally in order to prepare sermons, Bible studies, talks, etc. It gives a framework to approach God in the simplicity of faith and allow him to speak directly to us, rather than through the efforts of intellectual study.

Lectio divina can also be used in a group setting, although the contemplative aspect is normally omitted since by nature it is a more personal experience. For this, Norvene Vest in *Knowing by Heart* provides an excellent summary:

The basic process for our group lectio is roughly this:

(1) The leader reads a short passage from Scripture, and in silence the group members listen attentively for a particular word or phrase that seems to be given to each. Then each simply speaks aloud the word received.

---

[13] Richard Peace, *Contemplative Bible Reading* (NavPress, 1998), pp. 12–13. Used by permission of NavPress.

(2) Another member reads the same passage a second time, and in silence the group members ponder how the passage seems to touch their lives. Then each person briefly speaks aloud his or her sense of being touched.

(3) The same passage is read a third time, and in silence group members reflect on a possible invitation found in the passage to do or be something in the next few days. Each person speaks of the invitation he or she has received.

(4) Finally the group members each pray in turn that the person to his or her right be empowered to do or to be what he or she feels called to do or to be.[14]

Both Peace and Vest provide further helpful instructions about how to follow *lectio divina* effectively, both individually and in the context of a group. Peace suggests that in a postmodern context *lectio divina* will grow in popularity, as it offers an experiential alternative to a merely cognitive approach to Bible study.

One Sunday evening I was preaching in a local church. As the time drew near for me to speak, I grew more and more certain that I should not give the address I had prepared, but rather lead the congregation in a corporate *lectio divina* exercise. Knowing that as a group they were not afraid to try new things, I decided to follow what I felt was a prompting of the Holy Spirit. I explained that, rather than serving up yet another pre-cooked meal for them from God's word, I wanted to teach them how to hear God for themselves simply by listening to the reading of Scripture. That seemed to win their attention, for they realised they could not just sit back and listen to what I had to say about the passage – they would have to engage with it for themselves.

---

14 Norvene Vest, *Knowing by Heart* (DLT, 1995), pp. 4–5.

I chose a short passage from Psalm 27, and slowly read it to them three times. When opportunity came to share which words or phrases had impacted them most, several people immediately shared with the rest of the congregation. It was obvious that they were hearing from God – very clearly, very personally and also very easily. The minister of the church himself said that God had spoken to him through the words 'all the days of my life' (v.4). Afterwards he shared more fully with me.

Apparently he had just celebrated his fortieth birthday, a milestone in anyone's life, and was conscious of wanting to make the most of his life in service to God. Those simple words had impacted him at his point of need, and had become a means by which he was enabled again to offer himself and his service to God for the rest of his life. A simple but profound interaction with the word of God made possible by the reading of Scripture.

On most occasions when I have taken part in *lectio divina* myself, I have found that God has invariably spoken to me very clearly, and that I have had no difficulty in remembering what he said. Somehow it went straight to my heart. When I compare this to the number of sermons I have heard and soon forgotten, it makes me think I should be using *lectio divina* more often!

FOR REFLECTION

1. Take the following scripture (or another of your own choosing) and meditate on it: 'In him and through faith in him we may approach God with freedom and confidence' (Ephesians 3:12). Chew it over in your mind. Perhaps memorise it. What does it say to you? How does it apply to your life at this moment?

2. Try *lectio divina*, either by yourself or with others. Choose a passage that is fairly short and not too doctrinal – some examples might be: Isaiah 43:1–3; Matthew 11:28–30; Mark 1:35–37; Luke 5:4–7; John 15:15–16a; Ephesians 3:20–21. Remember, don't try to fathom the passage or to analyse its content. Simply listen to the scripture and allow the word to speak to you.

3. Try to get hold of a print of Rembrandt's 'The Return of the Prodigal Son' (most Christian bookshops will be able to locate one for you). Find a quiet place and meditate on the painting. What new insights come to you about the story? Which of the characters in the painting do you identify with, and why?

14

Contemplation

Contemplation is nothing else but a secret, peaceful infusion of God, which, if admitted, will set the soul on fire with the Spirit of love. (St John of the Cross)

A well-known story tells of a peasant who, every day after his work was completed, stopped to visit the village church on his way home. Leaving his pick-axe and spade outside, he would enter the church and sit in silence. Then, after about an hour, he would stand up and leave the church, continuing his way home.

The village priest had often watched the peasant from the back of the church, and one day, perplexed as to his purpose, approached the man.

'Why do you come into my church day after day, old man?' he asked. 'And why do you waste your time doing nothing when you are here?'

The old man looked at him. 'Sir,' he said humbly, 'I simply look at him and he looks at me, and we tell each other that we love each other.'

Contemplation has been defined as the gaze of the soul upon God. Others describe it as 'the prayer of loving attentiveness' or 'the prayer of loving regard'. In its essence it is about loving God and allowing ourselves to be loved by him.

To contemplate means to look steadily at. When we contemplate something we give it our full attention – whether it be a beautiful panorama, an arresting piece of music, a work of art or an aspect of nature. In Christian contemplation we are looking at Jesus and beholding or considering him. In silence and stillness we give attention to the one who is the Lover of our souls.

In biblical terms, contemplation is the experience of entering into the Most Holy Place; of drawing near to God and knowing him draw near to us. This, according to the letter to the Hebrews, is the reason Christ died: to bring us to God. No longer is God distant and remote. The curtain that separated us has been torn in two. We can come near with boldness and confidence.

Exactly where meditation ends and contemplation begins is not always clear. Many people use the terms interchangeably anyway, and in some ways they are almost inseparable. Yet there is a difference between them, and an important one. While meditation is like the journey, contemplation is like the arrival point. In meditating, we are seeking to make ourselves aware of God and to warm our hearts towards him. In contemplation, having already become aware of his presence, we are enjoying him, delighting ourselves in all that he is to us. Meditation helps us to reach the point at which contemplation begins. Meditation is part of the way, while contemplation (and delight in God) is the goal:

Contemplation goes further and deeper than meditation. While the person meditating mutters and muses on God's word, the contemplative pays silent attention to Jesus, the living Word – the one who is central to their prayer.[1]

It is easy to get the impression from some spiritual writings that contemplation is the high point in Christian experience, attainable by only a few fortunate individuals of the highest spiritual calibre. There is sometimes too sharp a distinction made between the 'active' way and the 'contemplative' way. Often the mystical aspects are over-emphasised, and analogies of ascent and an upward journey suggest that contemplation is hard work, reserved for a spiritual elite. A special kind of language and vocabulary is often used too, adding to the mystique and sense of exclusivity.

Alexander Ryrie, in his excellent book *Silent Waiting*, is quick to dismiss such an approach and to stress that contemplation is the provenance of all:

> Contemplative prayer . . . refers to the practice of praying silently rather than in words, of entering an inner silence and stillness in order to be open to God. This is a way of prayer which is available to all, regardless of how far up the spiritual mountain they may have climbed.[2]

Contemplation cannot be distinguished from prayer. Contemplation is prayer, and prayer is contemplation, but a particular form of prayer. In contemplative prayer we do not need to ask for anything. Petitionary prayer has its place, as does intercession, but contemplative prayer goes beyond asking God for things to the place where we simply rest in God.

---

[1] Joyce Huggett, *Learning the Language of Prayer* (BRF, 1994), p. 42.
[2] Alexander Ryrie, *Silent Waiting* (Canterbury Press, 1999), p. 4.

In it we ask for nothing – not even for any experience of God, for any progress in the spiritual life, for any growth in goodness, or for any benefit for ourselves or others – but we simply concentrate on God alone.[3]

Contemplative Prayer or contemplation: a prayer of heart and will which reaches out to God's presence. The lips and mind both come to rest: there is a simple gazing at the Lord while the heart reaches out without words and the will seeks to be one with God's will.[4]

Since God dwells in silence[5] it follows that our deepest relationship with him will be in and through silence. God does use words to communicate, but he is not bound by them. Indeed, human words remain inadequate for the deepest levels of communication, and often get in the way of what we are trying to say! God is able to communicate with us without words. The profoundest revelation often takes place not through conscious thought or mental agility, but simply by being with God. Ryrie again has a helpful comment:

His will or his word can become effective in us not only through the ideas of our heads but more profoundly through our being in his presence. God communicates most deeply through communion.[6]

---

[3] Alexander Ryrie, *Silent Waiting* (Canterbury Press, 1999), p. 164.

[4] Jim Borst, *Coming to God in Stillness* (Eagle), pp. 47–8.

[5] Ryrie says that 'God is silence' and that 'silence' is one way of describing the being of God, but I cannot agree with this. God may rightly be said to dwell in silence (the silence of eternity), but he is not to be confused with silence itself, nor is it one of his attributes. See Alexander Ryrie, *Silent Waiting* (Canterbury Press, 1999), p. 133.

[6] *Op cit.*, p. 133.

Perhaps this is one of the sticking points for those who are used to a more cerebral approach to understanding God. Contemplative spirituality is a spirituality of the heart, by which is meant not the seat of the emotions, but 'a person's inner centre, the seat and mainspring of the inner life, one's inmost and truest self'.[7] It represents the spiritual dimension of our being. God is to be apprehended not with mental faculties, but with spiritual ones; with what the apostle Paul called 'the eyes of your heart' (Ephesians 1:18). Contemplative writers often use such expressions as 'descending into the heart' or 'putting the mind into the heart'. What they mean is that in contemplating God the natural mind has its limitations. We cannot *know* God through intelligence, only *know about* God. Direct, first-hand, life-changing knowledge of God comes only through revelation, and that comes to the centre of a person – what the Bible calls the 'heart' (see 1 Corinthians 1:21).

It is important to remember at this point that contemplation is not actually something we do ourselves, unaided. We need the help of God. As Thomas Merton reminds us, 'True contemplation is not a psychological trick but a theological grace. It can come to us *only* as a gift.'[8] Merton, one of the most respected contemplative writers, regarded contemplation as the work of the Holy Spirit within us: a gift given to all God's children if they wished to receive it, and given with the purpose of intensifying our awareness of the love God has for us. He was convinced that the majority of Christians have no idea of the immensity of the love of God

---

[7] Alexander Ryrie, *Silent Waiting* (Canterbury Press, 1999), p. 165.

[8] Thomas Merton, *Contemplative Prayer*.

for them, or of the power of that love to do them good, to bring them happiness.

Contemplatives often speak of 'infused' prayer; that is, prayer that is poured into us by God and received as a gift. St Theresa, for example, stressed that contemplative prayer was divinely produced; a wordless awareness and love that can be neither initiated nor prolonged. It comes simply as a gift of grace. It is the love of God being shed abroad in our hearts by the Holy Spirit (Romans 5:5).

It is interesting to note the similarity between some descriptions of contemplative prayer ('an in-loveness felt and experienced') and the way in which some charismatics describe their experience of being baptised in the Spirit as 'falling in love with Jesus'. Certainly when I look back to the time when I was baptised in the Spirit, it was an experience of being overwhelmed by the love of God. I knelt in prayer by my bedside, hungry to know God more deeply, conscious of standing at the edge of a vast ocean, yet afraid to dip my toes in. It was his doing, not mine. It felt as if I had fallen backwards into the great ocean of God's love. I was wrapped and enveloped in a divine warmth of love and acceptance.

There have been other such times since then when God has come to me and I have felt his embrace. Without knowing the terminology, I was almost certainly experiencing this 'infused' prayer of which contemplatives speak. Perhaps there is a much closer overlap between charismatic experience and contemplative prayer than we may have realised, and that here is a meeting point between the two traditions.

This awareness that contemplation is a gift, rather than an art we have to learn, is extremely liberating, and makes what we are searching for attainable, since the initiative lies with God. It is not so much a matter of our finding God, but of our being found by him. It is not God who is elusive; we are!

> This is the nature of the encounter, not that I am stumbling towards Abba Father, but that the Abba Father is running towards me. It is not that I love God, but that God loves me; not that I believe in God, but that he believes in me. The discovery at the heart of contemplation is *not that I am contemplating the divine love, but that divine love is contemplating me*. God sees me and understands me, accepts me, has compassion on me, creates me afresh from moment to moment, and he protects me.[9]

These are profound words, which will repay careful meditation, for they open up before each of us the possibility of a new and deeper awareness of God and his love for us. It is not my love for God that is the mainspring of contemplative prayer, but his prior, unending and unchanging love for me! And while I may think of him at best intermittently, the thoughts he has towards me are without number, whether I wake or sleep (see Psalm 139:17–18).

Of course it means that there is an 'elusiveness' about contemplative prayer. Warm feelings are not always experienced, nor should they always be sought, or used as an indicator to gauge the worthwhileness of contemplative prayer. There is bound to be a natural ebb and flow in our apprehension of God, and there will inevitably be highs and lows. This is one reason why many contemplatives stress the need for discernment, and seek the help of a spiritual director or mentor – so that they are not discouraged when

---

[9] Bishop Stephen Verney, *Into the New Age* (Fontana, 1976), p. 91.

they have dry seasons, or feel abandoned when the warm glow disappears.

With this in mind, then, it is easier for us now to understand what true contemplation is: the response of our hearts to the call of God to rest in his presence and delight ourselves in his love. We draw near to him by relaxing ourselves and becoming quiet within. We hold ourselves in his presence, aware of the magnitude of his love towards us, leaning ourselves upon him and gazing upon his loveliness. There we remain, silent and content, not saying anything, happy to let him speak if he so desires.

Practical steps

By far the best practical guide I have found to contemplative prayer is *Coming to God in the Stillness* by Jim Borst. He suggests twelve steps we can follow as a method for contemplative prayer. For simplicity's sake I have reduced these to three phases but summarised the content of each step within these phases. It is assumed that anyone wishing to enter into contemplation will be unhurried as far as time is concerned. The feeling of being able to take as much time as necessary is more important than the actual amount of time available. The essential ingredient is to be focused and unhurried.

1. The beginning stage: relaxing

The first challenge is to quieten our hearts, following the call of God to be still and know that he is God (Psalm 46:10). We can do this by slowing ourselves down, breathing slowly and deeply, and relaxing our whole bodies. Next, with the encouragement of Scripture (1 Peter 5:7), we can hand over our tensions and worries to God, becoming aware that he is present with us. Consciously and deliberately we give to God the clutter of worries, anxieties and pressures that might keep us from prayer. We need to be honest and open about our feelings. We can only come to God as we are – as the hymn puts it, 'Just as I am . . .' Writing down how we are feeling may help to release us, and quiet, reflective music may help us unwind. It is important that we are authentic as we come to God. We can begin to call on the name of Jesus, or repeat the name 'Abba, Father'. Gradually our hearts will begin to open to God and we will begin to receive his love. It is important not to rush this stage, and some days we may need to spend the whole time at this point as we relax ourselves and allow the rest of God to enter us afresh.

2. The middle stage: drawing closer

Once we know our heart is awakened to God we can draw closer, beginning to deal with things that may hinder us from enjoying full communion with him. It may be appropriate to surrender ourselves to God afresh, asking that he would possess us anew. In particular it is important to come to an acceptance of God's will for our lives – the people, events, situations and conditions that surround us. We also need to forgive from the heart. God's mercy and grace flow freely towards us, and we should likewise forgive others. We let go of bitterness, resentment and hurt feelings, and anything else that God shows us is a barrier to our intimacy with him. We can repent to God of our own sin and failure in the knowledge that he forgives and accepts us, without us falling into either guilt or inferiority. At this point it is good to ask in faith that God would touch us afresh by his Spirit, seeking a personal anointing and a fresh outpouring of

God's love. On different occasions the Lord will emphasise different aspects of the process to us during this stage.
Again, the important thing is not to rush through them.

3. The final stage: enjoyment

As the barriers come down we find our hearts opening up
to God more fully, and we begin to experience the joy of
contemplation, when we are held enraptured by God.
Prayer has become nothing but a 'loving awareness' of him.
His presence is more and more real. He has our attention.
This phase may move in any of several directions. It may
become a time of receiving from God. It may move into
praise and thanksgiving. We may be led to intercede, feeling
God's heart for other people and the world. We may simply
stay resting in the presence of our Beloved One, basking in
the warmth of his love and approval.

It has often been said that the best way to learn how to pray
is to pray, and certainly the best way to learn how to contemplate is to contemplate. As we regularly open ourselves up to
God in this way it is bound to have a transforming effect on
our lives. We cannot enjoy intimacy with God like this and
remain unchanged. As Leslie Weatherhead described it,
Christ's friendship is a 'transforming friendship'.

We can expect to be more relaxed, more at peace and
more like Christ. We will be more aware of sin and have a
greater hatred for it. We will have a greater realisation that
we are loved by God, and as a result have a greater love for
other people. With time we can expect to become more
truly ourselves and have a greater freedom from the hang-
ups that have troubled us in the past. Hopefully there will
be a greater balance in our lives (between rest and work),
and we will enjoy our own company more. We may also

feel more invigorated for service, but less inclined to run around doing everything as we once did. Most importantly of all, we will be more pleasing to God.

Contemplation sets before us an exciting adventure, the possibility of exploring new depths in the love of God. This is what our souls were made for, what they cry out for and long for – to know God more deeply. This was the longing of King David, to see the beauty of the Lord. This was the heart cry of the apostle Paul, 'that I may know him'. It is the true yearning of all in whom the Spirit of God dwells, and 'who have set their hearts on pilgrimage' (Psalm 84:5).

FOR REFLECTION

1. Find a quiet place that is comfortable and where you can be alone. Relax yourself, either by listening to music that brings you into stillness, breathing slowly and deeply, or just becoming still. Hand your heart-aches and pressures to God. Then follow the steps towards contemplation outlined in this chapter. You will need to practise this several times until it becomes natural and easy. At first it may seem forced and artificial, but persevere. With time it will flow more easily.

2. Be aware that meditation quite naturally leads to contemplation, as does worship. Be ready for those moments when your spirit is touched and you can move naturally from thinking about God in your mind to contemplating him in your heart. Again, with practice you will learn to recognise such moments. When they come, be still, be silent. Relax, enjoy the presence of God. Behold his beauty.

3. Remember that contemplation is not first and foremost

about experiences. It is sufficient simply to have been still and quiet in God's presence, regardless of whether we have heard his voice or not. Even if we remain unmoved spiritually, it is still a worthwhile thing to do.

Living Freely and Lightly

Where to from here? If the Spirit really is calling us to an integration of contemplative spirituality within the activism of the evangelical and charismatic streams, what are the implications? The most significant seems to be that we must be able to work out our spirituality within the demands of modern life. Can busy people really be contemplative? Can we realistically incorporate silence and solitude into twenty-first-century lifestyles? Can we learn to live freely and lightly in this day and age?

To the Praying Heart

You have brought your heart here to be exposed to My love.
Each quiet, restful beat brings it closer and closer.
Your presence, like drifting incense, lingers before Me.

It is good for you to be here with Me.
You are not here to ask for anything. You are here just to be
    here,
letting our presences mingle and our wills focus into ONE.

When you leave My presence, others may ask:
'Where have you been, what fire has touched your soul?'
They will run from the chill of the world
to the warmth of the Hearth that warmed you.

Stay with Me in the silence and let us just be.

Angela Ashwin

15

Spirituality for Busy People

I began writing this book at the start of a three-month sabbatical from my work. I was looking forward to a time of concentrated study and some much needed peace and quiet. The first day of my leave coincided with the commencement of renovation work in the bathroom of our home. We expected it to last two weeks, and I felt I would be able to put up with the noise and some minor inconveniences for such a short time. Little did I realise all that could go wrong on such a project.

Three months later, as my leave came to an end, the bathroom was finally finished! There had been many disappointments, many frustrations and many hassles along the way. We had to contend with inadequate workmen, unexpected delays, leaking pipes and broken fittings. We were without central heating for ten days during a cold spell. The bathroom was unusable for days on end. A most stressful experience! If ever I thought my sabbatical would transport me to another dimension of heavenly living, I was wrong. But then that's what real life is all about, isn't it? And we must be able to work out our faith in the context of a real and often trying world.

Whatever form our spirituality takes, it has to be related to everyday life. It must be practical, and applicable by ordinary people in their normal situations. A rediscovery of contemplative spirituality offers the possibility of restoring balance and harmony to lives that are overcrowded and far too hectic. It must also, however, be integrated into the whole of life as it is lived in the day to day.

Some feel that contemplative spirituality holds the danger of being a 'spirituality of withdrawal'. While recognising the value of times of solitude and aloneness for the nurture of the spirit, they argue, quite rightly, that there must be a connection between this and the things that normally occupy and preoccupy the majority of us. They call for a 'domestic' spirituality, by which they mean a spirituality that can be expressed in the home and family, in the workplace and office:

> Spirituality is about all of life and all of who we are. It has to do with moments of retreat and rush-hour traffic, with periods of silence and the noise of little children, with the communion table and the work bench, with hushed Sunday worship and frantic family dinners.[1]

Peterson's paraphrase of John 1:14 lends weight to this point of view, illustrating graphically for us as it does the reality of Christ's incarnation and the depth of his identification with us: 'The Word became flesh and blood, and moved into our neighbourhood.' Jesus certainly practised times of 'strategic withdrawal' throughout his ministry, but he never cut himself off from people or their needs. He lived

---

[1] Simon Holt 'Finding God in the ordinary, the mundane, and the immediate', *Fuller* magazine, March 1999, p. 23.

his life before them in the cut and thrust of human existence, and he calls us to do the same. He could be seen, heard, touched. His teaching drew on imagery straight from the everyday lives of his hearers. It was no abstract, philosophical message he preached, but one soaked in the real concerns of ordinary people. The incarnation sets us free for divine encounters in the domestic settings of our lives.

It may be true, also, that contemplative spirituality can appear out of the reach of ordinary Christians who have little free time, but who need to concentrate on mundane things such as nappies, earning their living and simply keeping things going:

> The average Christian who lives out his or her faith in suburbia, employed in the marketplace and paying the mortgage, can often be led to gaze longingly at the pastor, missionary, or monk as the one who has chosen the higher path.[2]

Of course, this should not be so. In whatever context we live, we should be able to work out the terms of our discipleship in ways that are realistic and attainable. The parent with young children, the student with exams, the boss with his deadlines, the salesman on the road . . . each should be able to find a spirituality that works in their situation, and which draws them closer to God. That is not to say that it will be easy to do so. Perhaps the greatest hindrance is the fact that often we fail and are drawn back into our old ways so easily.

It is my conviction, however, that contemplative spirituality can be integrated into ordinary living. The pace of life

---

[2] Simon Holt 'Finding God in the ordinary, the mundane, and the immediate', *Fuller* magazine, March 1999, p. 15.

is not going to get slower, and many will need to experience God while travelling in the fast lane. But even there, God is to be found. Amid the pressures and the turmoil, the stress and the strain, we can encounter him as genuinely as in the most sacred cathedral. As Joyce Huggett says:

> The good news is that God can be found in the fast lane. His presence and his love are as available to us when we are besieged by busyness as they are when we pull into a quiet lay-by to contemplate him.[3]

So then, how can we find God in our busyness? And how can we integrate contemplative spirituality into the demands of modern living?

It will be helpful to *consider the level of our desire for God*. To find God we must want God. How badly do we want to know God? If our desire is currently low it may be because something or someone has taken the place of God in our lives. Adjustment may be necessary. Otherwise, we may need to ask God to increase the desire within us. In my experience, hunger for God makes room for itself. If we truly long for God we will make time for him, no matter how crowded our lives are.

Then we must be willing to undertake *a thoroughgoing re-evaluation of the way we live*. Hopefully the things we have considered so far have helped us to recognise the value and importance of silence and solitude, and of their significance for our well-being, both physically and spiritually. Without a radical shift in our values we will not have

---

[3] Joyce Huggett, *Finding God in the Fast Lane* (Eagle, 1993), p. 21. I am indebted to Joyce for many of the thoughts expressed in this chapter.

the willingness to change established behaviour patterns. However, if we are convinced it is essential to find time and space for God, and to build periods of reflection into our lives, then there is the hope that even in our busy schedules we may find room.

It will also be good to review *how we are using our time*, and to ask ourselves some searching questions. Why am I so busy? What drives me to attend so many meetings? Is my workaholic tendency covering up some underlying issue that I am afraid to face? Whose approval am I seeking in all my activity? What am I trying to prove? Above all, we need to ask the question 'Is there anything I could prune from my diary?' If we are willing to be radical we may well find that we have more time and space available to us than we realised, and our lives may become less cluttered and more easily managed.

It may also be timely to *consider our image of God, and the basis on which we relate to him*. How do we think of God? Do we see him as an ever-demanding Employer, paying low wages and demanding long hours? Or is he some despotic Pharaoh, asking us to make bricks without straw and treating us like slaves? Is he a God who is never satisfied, never pleased with us, never smiling? Even mature Christians can live with distorted ideas of God.

In order to make time for God we need to want to be with him. If we understand what he is truly like, we shall long for his presence. Remember, God is full of intense love towards us and only wants to do good in our lives. He welcomes us unconditionally and desires the very best for us. He is full of mercy and grace, and would do nothing to hurt or harm us. He is our Shepherd, Saviour and Friend, and longs to be with us.

We are to relate to God on the basis of his grace towards

us. I can come to him just as I am and know that I will be welcomed and accepted. Even if I have failed and not lived up to my own best standards, I can still draw near. I don't have to earn my acceptance or achieve the right to be there. I can come boldly and confidently because God himself has provided a way by which I can draw near to him. I come, not on the basis of my own goodness (I have none anyway), but on the basis of my position in Christ.

Strategies for finding God

Having undertaken a review like this we can now build into our lives certain strategies that will help us to experience God more frequently in the midst of the maelstrom of life.

1. We can find God as we learn to 'practise the presence of God'

We associate this expression with Brother Lawrence. He was a seventeenth-century monk in France who found himself, somewhat reluctantly, assigned to kitchen duties on a regular basis. Rather than complaining, however, he gave himself wholeheartedly to the task of serving God where he was, and right there among the pots and pans he learned to 'practise the presence of God'. So remarkable was his serenity in the midst of the steamy kitchens that he became a celebrity, with both rich and famous coming to meet him and learn the secret of his peacefulness. It was, of course, the fact that he was constantly aware of God's presence with him, even as he did the washing-up, that brought such calmness to his spirit:

God is everywhere, in all places and there is no spot where we cannot draw near to him, and hear him speaking in our heart: with a little love, just a very little, we shall not find it hard.[4]

What Brother Lawrence discovered in the kitchens, we can find on the shop floor, in the nursery or in the classroom. God is with us wherever we are and whatever we are doing, and at any moment we can enter into dialogue with him. Busy days can be filled with his presence. Earthly stables can become his dwelling place.

We live in a God-bathed world. There is no place where God is not, although sometimes we may be asleep to his presence. This is why we need what writer Timothy Jones calls 'awakenings'.[5] These are divinely given moments in our day when we become aware of the activity and nearness of God. Suddenly, in the midst of another humdrum day, we see the traces of divine presence. It may be in words that are spoken, an incident that takes place, a thought that comes to us, something that makes us laugh or cry . . . suddenly we are aware of God. He is in the moment. The more 'awake' we become, the more we recognise that our days contain many such moments, many such glimpses of the divine. All we need are eyes to see: 'The whole of life as it is lived is seized by God's vital power and is lived *"before God"* because it is lived *"out of God"*.'[6] God is there already in the dailyness of living. He has impregnated our world with himself. What we need is to be attentive to him. His presence needs to be realised.

---

[4] Brother Lawrence, quoted by Joyce Huggett, *Finding God in the Fast Lane* (Eagle, 1993), p. 28.

[5] Timothy Jones, *Awake My Soul* (Doubleday, 1999).

[6] Möltmann, quoted by Simon Holt 'Finding God in the ordinary, the mundane, and the immediate', *Fuller* magazine, March 1999, p. 15.

2. We can find God in the world around us

The Celtic Christians were particularly alive to the presence of God. For them life was lived in the atmosphere of God's nearness. Whether milking the cow or copying the Scriptures, all was divine activity, all was sacred. Everything took place within the overshadowing presence of God. The Lord was there all around them in the beauty of nature – in the seas and skies, in the fish and the birds, in the mountains and coastlines. All spoke of him, and they heard his voice. For them there was no distinction between sacred and secular. God was all and in all.

We need to rediscover this holistic approach to life, for God is more present in our own sophisticated world than we imagine. The world around us offers plenty of opportunity to encounter God. As the children's hymn says, 'This world is like a picture book to tell his love to me.' How often do we stop to read it? It is there all around us, declaring the glory of God.

> It is such a very simple thing to walk through life with my hands open, my eyes open, listening, alive in all my five senses to God breaking in again and again on my daily life.[7]

Such a possibility is open to us all. Even as we travel around in the midst of our busyness, we can see the handiwork of God. In the city centre it is there – in the trees, the birds, the people, the colours, the sky, the rain, the bricks, the shape of the buildings . . . 'Wherever I live, whatever the time of year, what I see, taste, and touch can

---

[7] Esther de Waal, quoted by Timothy Jones, *Awake My Soul* (Doubleday, 1999), p. 68.

point my soul, if I let it, to a new awareness of God's creative goodness.'[8]

3. We can find God as we sanctify our work

Whatever work we are given to do (whether paid or volun-
tary, at home or elsewhere) we can see it as our calling, and
do it for the glory of God. Such an attitude transforms our
work and brings God right into the centre of our lives. After
all, most of our time is taken up with work in one form or
another, and it is unthinkable to leave God out of such a
major part of our lives. If I know I am doing it for him, that
it is as much 'service' as any spiritual form of activity – my
work is dignified, and I can feel his pleasure in what I do:
'The simplest labour is no less special; God eagerly employs
all work done with conscience and commitment. He enlists
it all into his great purpose.'[9]

We can also expect to see God at work within our work.
He will use the circumstances of our work to shape and
mould our character, for he is just as much sovereign over
what happens there as anywhere else. No moment of our
day, and no part of our life, is outside of his control. And
of course we can bring God into our working environment
by thinking of him and praying quietly, as we get the opportunity. He is interested in the details of our work, since anything that is a concern to us is a concern to him. We
can pray as much about our work as about our church
activities. Thomas Kelly called this 'living concurrently',
keeping one eye on heaven while being firmly engaged on
earth:

---

[8] Timothy Jones, *Awake My Soul* (Doubleday, 1999), p. 70.
[9] *Ibid.*, p. 133.

I find that a life of little whispered words of adoration, of praise, of prayer, of worship can be breathed all through the day. One can have a very busy day, outwardly speaking, and yet be steadily in the holy Presence.[10]

It may not be easy to maintain such a spiritual orientation, but it is possible. We can soak our work with our prayer. In this way, our work can be our worship, as we offer what we do to God, and as we seek to remain aware of him throughout the day.

4. We can find God as we learn to pace ourselves

Enjoying the presence of God has to do with leaving spaces in our lives; with not overcrowding ourselves. This is partly to do with good planning and partly to do with creating an appropriate rhythm in our lives. It is important that we find patterns that fit us rather than establish rigid systems. After all, we are seeking to nurture a relationship with a Person, not run a programme. We need to under-stand how we function best – what works for us and what doesn't:

We consider our natural alternations: Work and rest. Action and prayer. Intimacy and solitude. We remember how one feeds the other. How one drives the other. We move in and out as our lives and our souls require.[11]

It is rather like a large wheel with a hub at the centre. Part of us (the rim) is in touch with the ground; that is, the ordinary demands of daily life. This is the part that is moving. The hub, however, is at the centre and remains

---

[10] Thomas Kelly, *A Testament of Devotion* (Harper, 1941), p. 120.
[11] Timothy Jones, *Awake My Soul* (Doubleday, 1999), p. 112.

still. This is our heart, or spirit, which is in tune with God. Thus we combine both busyness and stillness. Our activities revolve around a still axis, and this is what creates balance and harmony in our lives.

In this context I have found particularly helpful the insights of David Kundtz in his book *Stopping*.[12] He describes three ways of being still even when we have to keep going. He calls them stillpoints, stopovers and grinding halts.

Even the busiest of lives has its quiet moments, its stillpoints. We have to recognise them and make use of them. Coffee breaks, lunch hours, travelling time and walking between offices can all provide us with little moments of solitude that can nourish our soul. Sometimes we have to choose to leave the crowd and be alone. These little pools of silence, 'kingdom moments' as Joyce Huggett calls them, are given by God so that we can turn our hearts towards him. They take us from the rim to the hub.

Many people find it helpful to more deliberately frame their day with a short period (say 15 minutes) for quiet meditation and prayer. This regular pattern helps to establish within them a 'still centre' out of which they can operate for the rest of the day. It gives a focus to their lives and helps them set priorities. From this place of rest within themselves they can respond more efficiently to the chaos around them.

Sometimes a group of friends with a shared desire for God can arrange to meet together. I am fortunate to have the opportunity to attend such a group that meets weekly during the lunch hour. After a short time of devotion, often using a simple liturgy, we have 20 minutes of quiet,

---

[12] David Kundtz, *Stopping* (Newleaf, 1998).

contemplative prayer. I doubt if I would manage that on my own, but with the encouragement of others, and the framework provided by those who host the meeting, I am able to find an opportunity for stillness in the midst of my normally busy timetable. Meeting with others is also a valuable antidote against becoming too individualistic in one's relationship with God.

As well as daily times of stillness, we will need to be renewed through more leisurely periods of quiet. These are the stopovers, and can be achieved with careful forethought and determination. We need to commit ourselves to it – not leave it as some vague good intention for when the time is right. It will never be right! A day away on our own can provide much needed space. Parents with small children can make a 'gift' of such a day to each other occasionally. Such opportunities are like an oasis when you have a small family. It has even been suggested that parents can take it in turns to be first Mary, then Martha!

Longer periods – the grinding halts – may be taken for retreat as well, realising that such 'time away' is not a luxury but a necessity. Here we are thinking of two or three days at a time, and even longer for those who have the appetite and desire. These are not the extravagances of a selfish life, but the essentials for a balanced one. Holidays were originally meant to be holy days, and if we bear this in mind it may well be possible for some of us to use our time off work to enrich our walk with God. It is worth reflecting too that God in his love has a way of making us take enforced rest from time to time as well. If we won't commit ourselves to do it, we may well find such rest imposed on us through sickness or other circumstances.

The principle of the sabbath still holds good, and we neglect it at our spiritual and emotional peril. Many of those who have suffered burnout thought they were exempt! If God was concerned for the ground to lie fallow, how much more is he concerned that we his children have proper rest and recreation, and the chance to be still? So we incorporate into our hectic schedules pauses when we can spend time at the hub, receiving a fresh inflow of divine life. We learn to pace ourselves.

A friend decided to take a day for prayer and fasting, hoping to combine it with his work responsibilities. He managed the fasting, but unfortunately that particular day was fraught with unexpected difficulties and demands, and he failed to pray. He was disappointed, feeling he had let himself and God down. Such an experience illustrates the difficulty of finding a spirituality that works for busy people.

What my friend failed to appreciate, however, was that he was thinking of prayer in a limited way – either as vocal prayer or as prayer formed in the mind. He perhaps failed to realise that God reads our hearts and knows our desires, whether or not we manage to express them outwardly. Prayer is not just an activity that we do; it is a relationship that we live, an attitude of our heart. Because he was living within the presence of God his prayer was heard, because *he is his prayer*. God knows the desires of our heart.

My drive to work lasts just over half an hour. I am grateful for this oasis of calm as I move into the day, and then as I move out of it in the evening on my way home. Sometimes I listen to the radio, sometimes I think about work-related issues, but often now I spend part of the time singing praise to God. It is not a legalistic practice, nor is it a duty that I feel I must perform. It seems to be just the natural expression of the life of God within me, and it has become a special time for me. It is one of the rhythms of grace that the Spirit has helped me to build into my own life, and it helps to keep me centred on Jesus and abiding in him. Nothing profound or revolutionary, just a simple habit in the midst of an ordinary day.

This is what contemplative spirituality is all about, and it works, even in the busiest of lives.

FOR REFLECTION

1. Given the demands upon you, how can you work out a 'domestic' spirituality? What changes can you make that will help you become more contemplative? What are the limitations upon you that you will have to accept and work within for the time being?

2. To find God you must want God. Ask yourself, 'Do I really want him?' If you do, ask yourself, 'Do I have to be this busy? Is there something I can let go of? Can I plan my time better? Do I have the right priorities?'

3. Think of practical steps you can take to integrate some of the aspects of contemplative spirituality into your life. Write them down. Do something about them.

16
The Dream

I had been speaking at a conference on the south coast of England, and after one of the sessions was talking informally with a delegate who shared with me something of her own story, and how God had been helping her to live in the rhythms of grace. God had spoken to her quite profoundly through a dream, and as a result she had made significant changes to her whole way of life, and especially her pattern of work. I was so moved by what she shared with me that I asked her permission to share her story with others. Here, in her own words, Beverley Shepherd explains what happened, how she responded and the challenge it presents to us all.

*   *   *

We all dream – or so I'm told. It's just that I don't normally remember mine. So when, in August 1999, I awoke with every detail of a dream vividly etched on my memory, I knew that God had spoken . . .

The dream concerned a rail journey. I was travelling by train to a large city, arriving at one terminus and then needing to continue my journey from a second terminus some way across the city. Bicycles were provided to cross the city, but I had only three minutes to make my connection. I pedalled furiously, while clutching a parcel containing something very precious. Worn out, I arrived at the second terminus with time to spare, but had lost the parcel! Still, with my 30 remaining seconds I could retrace my journey and find it – or so I thought. The precious parcel had disappeared and in its place I collected several other parcels – all jiffy bags full of bubble wrap.

I dashed back to the second terminus and leaped onto the train as it was pulling out of the station. Making my way to a corner seat I collapsed, exhausted and surrounded by my parcels full of nothing. It was then that I awoke.

I knew that the dream had been a warning. 'What was in that first parcel that was so precious?' was my anxious question as I prayed. God showed me. I picked up my diary and started to arrange my schedule. My diary is not that easy to reorganise, with many events being booked several months in advance. Six months later the changes started to bear fruit and I realised with both shock and gratitude that God's warning had come just in time.

The changes I made to my diary reflected the principles of 'working from rest' – of building into my life weekly, monthly and yearly patterns and starting each of these cycles with times of drawing aside to listen to God. That listening involves discerning his priorities and perspective on the work and relationships I am called to, but first and foremost it is the time when I remember who I am: his beloved daughter in whom he is well pleased. Everything flows from that understanding.

What might you lose if you continue to live at your present pace? Your laughter and spontaneity? Your sense of fun? Your peace? Your vision? Your most cherished relationships? Your intimacy with God?

Only you know, and only you can choose to change.

*   *   *

As God speaks, perhaps through the pages of this book, and calls you back to intimacy with himself, it is up to you to respond and take up his gracious invitation. Then, when you come to him, you will discover what true rest is, and you too will start to recover your life. You will learn from Jesus the unforced rhythms of grace, and as you practise them, you will begin to live freely and lightly.

Discipline of Intimacy

by Charlie Cleverly

Every believer may long for intimacy with God, but how do we attain to it? More importantly, how do we cultivate a life that is characterised by it?

'A beautifully written, easily digestible, biblically based inspiration to press on in prayer. Charlie Cleverly offers us a timely classic.'

Bishop David Pytches

'I had to put the book down and get alone with God.'

John Arnott, Toronto Airport Christian Fellowship

'Very moving, practical, helpful, inspiring.'

Sandy Millar, Vicar, Holy Trinity Brompton

'It will change your life as you read it . . . this is recommended reading.'

John Mulinde, World Trumpet Mission, Uganda

CHARLIE CLEVERLY was pastor of a French-speaking church in inner-city Paris for ten years, but has now returned to the UK to become Rector of St Aldate's Church, Oxford. He is married to Anita and they have four children.

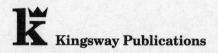 **Kingsway Publications**